THE
10TH
MOUNTAIN
HUT BOOK

A winter guide to Colorado's
10th Mountain and Summit hut systems
near Aspen, Vail, Leadville and Breckenridge

Warren Ohlrich

WHO PRESS ■ BASALT, COLORADO

Dedicated to Fritz Benedict and all the other soldiers of the 10th Mountain Division

© 2006 by Warren H. Ohlrich

PUBLISHED BY

WHO Press
Basalt, CO 81621
www.whopress.com

Library of Congress Control Number: 2005936122
ISBN 978-1-882426-23-2

All photos by Warren H. Ohlrich unless otherwise indicated
Cover design and maps by Curt Carpenter
Edited by Warren H. Ohlrich

Printed in the United States of America

Contents

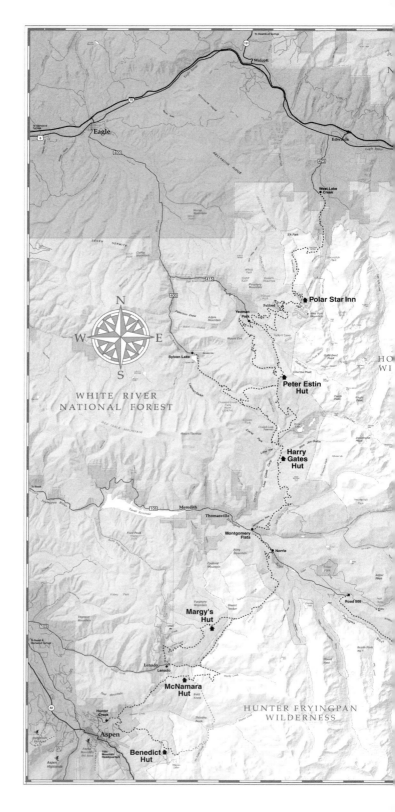

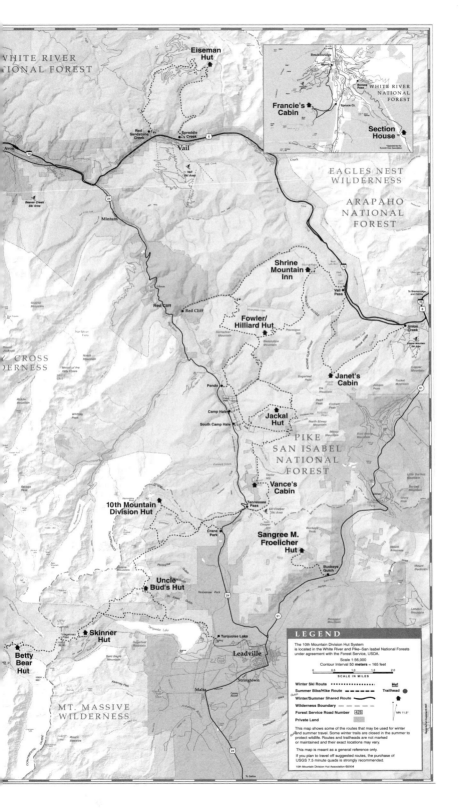

WHITE RIVER
ATIONAL FOREST

Eiseman
Hut

Breckenridge

Boreas
Pass

WHITE RIVER
NATIONAL
FOREST

Francie's
Cabin

Spruce Cr.

Section
House

*Operated by the
Summit Hut Association

Red
Sandstone
Creek

Spraddle
Creek

6

Vail

Vail
Ski Area

24

Beaver Creek
Ski Area

Avon

70

Minturn

EAGLES NEST
WILDERNESS

ARAPAHO
NATIONAL
FOREST

70

Shrine
Mountain
Inn

Vail
Pass

8

Union
Creek

Copper Mountain Ski Area

Red Cliff   Red Cliff

Fowler/
Hilliard Hut

91

Janet's
Cabin

CROSS
DERNESS

Pando

Camp Hale

South Camp Hale

Jackal
Hut

PIKE
SAN ISABEL
NATIONAL
FOREST

Vance's
Cabin

10th Mountain
Division Hut

Tennessee
Pass

Ski Cooper
Ski Area

Crane
Park

Sangree M.
Froelicher
Hut

Buckeye
Gulch

Uncle
Bud's Hut

24

91

Skinner
Hut

Betty
Bear
Hut

Turquoise Lake

Leadville

Stringtown

MT. MASSIVE
WILDERNESS

Malta

24

To Salida

Preface

The winter huts covered in this book are the huts in the 10th Mountain Division Hut Association and Summit Huts Association systems. These huts are all booked by the 10th Mountain Division Hut Association and will be collectively referred to as the "10th Mountain Hut System".

The 10th Mountain Hut System in the Colorado mountains around Aspen, Vail, Leadville, and Breckenridge is the finest and most popular winter hut system in the country. Visiting the 10th Mountain huts in the winter can be one of the most rewarding experiences in a person's life. Many hutgoers have even gone so far as to say that their trip has been a life-changing experience. Making a hut trip can test an individual both mentally and physically, rewarding him with a new sense of accomplishment. It is also a time to make new friendships, test one's decision-making abilities, and create a new perspective on the world.

But a winter hut trip can also be a bad experience for the unprepared. The weather in the mountains of Colorado can change quickly from glorious sunshine to a winter blizzard. After new snows, route finding can be very difficult. The physically unprepared can be in for a rough trip when they have to break trail or climb several thousand feet in elevation at high altitudes. Equipment problems can be a headache. At times, poor decisions create a situation where the hutgoer has to spend the night out in the snow and cold.

The primary purpose in writing this guidebook is to make the hut experience a memorable one, an experience that will be safe and add to the quality of the hutgoer's life. The 10th Mountain huts are the best in the country; the Colorado high country is known for its beauty; the chance for healthy exercise while backcountry skiing to and around the huts in this setting is unique. This guidebook will give you what you need to safely travel the path to that memorable and life-changing experience.

Acknowledgments

A number of people have been extremely helpful in getting together the information for this book. I would like to thank Ben Dodge and the 10th Mountain Division Hut Association staff for all the support, information, and helping make the many hut research trips possible on short notice. Thanks especially to Scott Messina of 10th Mountain for answering route questions that kept coming up. Thanks also to Lou Dawson, with whom I worked on publishing his guidebook to the 10th Mountain Hut System. I've learned a lot from him about winter guidebooks, and have used his guide extensively on my own trips.

It would have been much more difficult and dangerous to do the many trips alone as I retraced all the routes to all the huts this past winter. Special thanks to my companions Ann Jeffrey and Kristine Tracz who helped break trail, provided another set of eyes to stay on course, and put up with all my gathering of information on my recorder and GPS. Thanks also to Stan Wagon for accompanying me on day trips to a couple of the huts and for providing valuable information. Thanks to my son Miles for the wonderful trip over Hagerman Pass. Most of all, thanks to my wife, Karen, for not only going along on some of the trips, but also for putting up with my being gone in the mountains for half of this past winter. Without her continual support and help, I could not have put this all together.

10th Mountain Hut System

Brief History

Backcountry ski huts started evolving from backcountry shelters to linked hut systems in Europe in the 1860s. The Haute Route, which crosses the Alps, is a familiar name to mountaineers and backcountry travelers throughout the world. In North America, mountain huts sprang up in Canada and the northeast United States. The first hut in the Appalachian Mountain Club Hut System was built in 1888. The ski hut idea in Colorado had its origin with the Tagert Hut near Aspen. This miner's cabin, used as a ski hut in the 1940s, became the nucleus of a collection of huts in the Elk Mountain Range above Ashcroft near Aspen, eventually known as the Alfred A. Braun Hut System.

During World War II, the ski troops of the 10th Mountain Division were trained at Camp Hale near Leadville, Colorado, and were sent to Italy toward the end of the war, playing a critical role in the battle at Riva Ridge. Many of the veterans returned to the Rocky Mountains after the war and became instrumental in establishing ski areas throughout Colorado and the West. One of the veterans, the architect Fritz Benedict, was thrown together with Ben Eiseman, a Haute Route traveler, and Robert McNamara, and avid skier and former Secretary of Defense. Under their auspices, two huts were built in 1982, the McNamara and Margy's huts, under permits by the U. S. Forest Service. These huts soon became a part of the newly formed 10th Mountain Division Hut Association. Other huts soon followed, with the goal of creating a hut link between Aspen, Vail, and Leadville being achieved by the turn of the century. Today the 10th Mountain Division Hut Association takes reservations for its own huts, the huts of the Summit Huts Association and the Alfred A. Braun Hut System, and the Friends Hut. See the 10th Mountain website www.huts.org for more details on the history of the huts.

10th Mountain Website (www.huts.org)

The 10th Mountain Division Hut Association has an extensive website with detailed information on on the huts and history of the huts, hut amenities, rates, capacities, how to make a reservation, hut availability, avalanche information, trailheads, shuttle services, guide services, copies of waivers, emergency information, hut etiquette, and much more. This guidebook does not try to repeat most of the information which is already on the website, only what is of primary importance, or is necessary on the trip.

Trip Planning Checklist (see website for more details)

1. Obtain a winter brochure from 10th Mountain. Join 10th Mountain to get their newsletter and early booking privileges.

2. Review potential routes and trips in the brochure and guidebook. Select the appropriate routes and huts for your group. Carefully evaluate the backcountry skills of the members of your group and pick a trip suited to the ability level of the least skilled and least fit person in the group. You should consider arranging for a guide, or make sure you have experienced winter backcountry travelers in your group.

3. Designate a group leader to coordinate the trip and reservations. Make reservations using the lottery system, your membership privileges, or the website.

4. Purchase the appropriate topographic maps (with the marked routes) from 10th Mountain for the trip you have planned.

5. Decide which trailheads to use and arrange car shuttles if necessary.

6. Get in good physical shape! Remember you will be going long distances at high altitudes in the cold. Keeping healthy and fit is one of the most important prerequisites for your hut trip.

7. Use the suggested equipment list to check out and acquire the necessary equipment for the trip.

8. Coordinate food with the other members of the group.

9. Return the signed waivers to 10th Mountain before the trip.

10. Leave your trip itinerary and date and time of return with someone, so that in case of an emergency you can be located; or, if you do not come out at the appointed time, they can locate you.

11. Take along your confirmation letter and hut combinations.

Guidebook Usage

The 10th Mountain Hut Book is primarily intended to be used as a guide for a well-planned and safe trip. The bulk of the book concentrates on giving detailed information on the routes from the trailheads to the huts, and on locating the trailheads. The book also summarizes the key information for trip planning, the basic hut procedure, and the essentials of winter navigation. Important lists in the back include emergency contacts, hut and trailhead GPS data, a directory of contacts, and an equipment checklist. The maps in the book are only to be used for general reference and trip planning. For the route information in the book to be useful and effective, it should be used with a 10th Mountain Hut System topographic map. This guidebook only covers the routes and huts for the 10th Mountain Division Hut Association and the Summit Huts Association. The more avalanche-prone Alfred A. Braun Hut System and the Friends Hut are well covered in Lou Dawson's book, *Colorado Backcountry Skiing, Volume I.*

Chapter: Each chapter covers one hut. The individual routes under each hut/chapter cover the routes from the available trailheads to the hut, and the routes to other huts from the hut being described in the current chapter. Trailhead and route information is put together on adjoining pages without unnecessary cross-references, so that they can be photocopied and easily brought along on the trip. However, separate maps and navigation equipment are a must. The routes in this guide are the basic 10th Mountain suggested and marked routes for most hut travelers, and are routed to avoid most avalanche hazards. Very experienced hut users sometimes choose alternate routes, but they must be expert winter mountaineers with exceptional navigation skills.

Difficulty: Beginner, intermediate, and advanced. The rating involves a combination of factors, including skiing skills, navigational difficulty, and distance/elevation gain.

Distance: All distances are one-way.

Time: This is only a very general guide for the time and is an average time. Fresh snow, severe weather, and poor visibility can all greatly increase the time required to do these trips. Having to break trail all the way to the hut usually doubles the time required to get there. Poor snow conditions, such as heavy snow, can also greatly increase the time required to cover the distance.

Text Map: These maps are for general reference only, and do not serve as useable trail maps.

10ᵗʰ Mountain Map: This map, obtainable from the 10ᵗʰ Mountain office, is a necessity for all routes.

USGS Map: A separate USGS topographic map is not always necessary in addition to the 10ᵗʰ Mountain Map, but the USGS map can be useful for GPS coordinate grids and for side trips by experienced hutgoers.

Elevation Gain/Loss: Great elevation gains require a greater degree of fitness; large elevation losses usually require more skiing expertise.

Notes: The notes give helpful information pertinent to a particular route.

Directions to Trailhead: Trailheads (where you park and get started) aren't always easy to find, so detailed directions are given for the drive to the trailhead. This section includes the elevation and GPS coordinates for the trailhead. Over a period of time, some trailhead locations are moved or are subject to snow plowing, so check the 10ᵗʰ Mountain website for any updates.

Route Description: For safety sake, descriptions of the routes are given in great detail, especially for critical junctions. GPS coordinates are also listed for those junctions which are important or easy to miss. Directions of the compass are given in capital letters (eg. N, W, SSE, SW, etc.) for clarity and to save space.

Winter Navigation

Undoubtedly the most critical part of any hut trip is getting to the hut safely from the trailhead, and getting from one hut to another safely without getting lost. Navigation in the Colorado high backcountry is a skill that must be carefully learned. Many factors affect the process, weather being the most obvious. After a fresh snow there are no tracks to follow. Visibility can be very poor during a snowstorm, especially above timber line. Cold can make you anxious to keep moving and sometimes causes you to make poor decisions. I have come across many hutgoers who have spent the night in the woods due to having trouble finding the trail, or underestimating the time it takes to make the trip to the hut.

Here are some of the basics of winter navigation to the huts:

1. Preparation. Spend time before you go on your hut trip to study your maps, guidebook, and any other information you might have for your route. If you use a GPS, mark the grid lines ahead of time on your 10th Mountain map. Check the 10th Mountain website for notes on avalanche danger and for changes in trailhead information. Be prepared! These are not trips to be taken lightly.

2. Maps. Have a good 10th Mountain topographic marked map that shows the routes and the hut locations. Know how to read the maps and the topographic lines. If you use a GPS at all, mark the UTM grids on the map if they are not already on it. A USGS quad can also be handy, as it has latitude and longitude markings.

3. Guidebook. Have a good guidebook (like this one) that describes the route you are taking. The guidebook can make you aware of critical intersections and what to expect on your trip. It will give you an idea as to how much time the trip will take, and point out trouble spots. Another person's prior experience can help make your trip a lot easier.

4. Compass and altimeter. These are indispensable tools to go along with the maps. Make sure you have a compass with the magnetic deviation set for Colorado. If you have a good GPS, you can use it for elevation readings.

5. GPS (global positioning system). A GPS is not necessary and should not be used for general navigation. Use the map, compass, and altimeter. However, if you know how to use a GPS, it can be helpful as a backup when you are not sure exactly where you are. It can also be helpful in locating critical trail intersections that are listed in this book. The book gives GPS data for trailheads, huts, and critical intersections using the WGS84 Datum. My field experience in this part of Colorado has shown that to transfer a reading from a GPS using the WGS84 Datum to a USGS topographic map using the 1927 North American Datum it is necessary to subtract 200 meters N and add 30 meters E to the GPS reading to get the map reading.

6. Trail markers. The 10th Mountain uses blue diamonds (in non-wilderness areas) and trail blazes (in wilderness areas) to help mark the 10th Mountain suggested routes. However, you should not depend on these markers to lead you; they are best used to confirm that you are on the right route. Your map, compass, and altimeter are still the best navigation tools. Also, trail blazes sometimes mark routes other than 10th Mountain routes, so coordinate what you see marked with what your map shows. Following ski tracks and snowmobile-packed roads may seem helpful, but many times they lead you off the correct trail.

7. Map reading. Pay very close attention to the route on your map. Take your time at critical intersections to make sure you are on the right route. Missing a turn and going an hour or two out of the way has caused many hutgoers to either spend the night out, or turn back.

8. Get an early start. During the winter months, especially December and January, the daylight hours are short. Try to plan to get to the huts in the early afternoon to allow for problems which may come up and delay you along the way. Navigation in the dark can be very difficult, so start early!

9. Stay together and pace yourselves. Be prepared to help any members of the group who are having problems. The combined assets of the group can be of great help to those in trouble.

10. Always have a backup plan if you are having trouble getting to the hut. First of all, you should be prepared to spend the night out in the woods, if necessary. Better yet, have options to turn back and return to where you came from if you see that you will not be able to make the hut by nightfall. Remember, breaking trail in fresh snow often doubles the time it takes to get to a hut.

Hut Procedures

Heating: Generally, all of the huts have a wood stove for heating and a wood cook stove. In most instances, the wood stove is sufficient to keep the hut warm. Please, only use the stove when necessary so as to conserve wood and not get the hut too warm. When starting the fire the damper should be open and kept open until a good hot fire with coals has developed. At that time the damper can be closed (on most stoves) to conserve fuel and to throw out more heat. Leave firewood stacked and ready for the next group in the hut.

Water: In almost all of the huts, water is obtained by melting snow in a big pot on top of the wood stove. When filling buckets with snow, be sure to get fresh snow from open areas (not from under trees) and a little away from the hut itself. If sediment and floaters get bad in the snowmelt pot, clean it out when it is at a low level, so as to have better water available for the next group comeing in. Many people drink water straight from the pot, but it is best to boil or filter your drinking water. In many huts a cistern hand pump at the sink provides water which can be used for dishes, but not for drinking (unless filtered), since it comes from melted water off the roof. Always leave a full pot of water for the next group.

Cooking: All of the huts now have propane gas burners for cooking. The burners use a timer which must be turned on before they can be lit. In addition, the cook stove can be used, especially if the oven is needed, or more heat in the hut is needed (which is usually not the case). Be aware that not all groups in the hut can be cooking at the same time, so plan your time and meals accordingly. See the website for the amenities in each hut.

Electricity: Most of the huts have a photovoltaic system for lighting; some use propane gas. Lights should be used very sparingly, since the storage batteries can get low quickly on cloudy days. There is no electricity available for any other use than lighting, except in a couple of the private huts. Check the website for more information on a particular hut.

Sleeping: Cots and bunks with mattresses and pillows are provided in each hut, so it is only necessary to bring a sleeping bag and pillow case. Quiet hours are 10 p.m. to 6 a.m. Take special care not to disturb those who are trying to get a good night's sleep.

Outhouses: All toilet facilities are stocked with toilet paper. Observe the posted rules for the composting toilets.

Cleaning: Hut chores that should be shared by the groups staying in the hut include getting snow for water, shoveling the decks and stairs after a fresh snow, chopping wood to keep a good supply available, washing dishes after eating to make room for the next group to cook, keeping things neat and out of the way of the other groups. When leaving, use the following checklist to leave a clean and ready hut for the next group: 1. Leave a full pot of water. 2. All dishes should be clean and put away. 3. Make sure the fire has burned down and take the ashes from the stove outside to the ashes barrel. 4. Turn off the photovoltaic system and gas burners. 5. Straighten up the beds. 6. Take all the trash out with you. Do not leave any food items behind. 7. Sweep the floors. 8. Shovel the decks and walkways. 9. Lock the hut.

Safety and Emergencies

Hopefully, you will never get into an emergency situation on your hut trip, but you must be prepared. The Colorado backcountry is very unforgiving and isolated from easy help. The first step in staying safe is to be prepared for what could happen on a hut trip to create an emergency situation.

Acute Mountain Sickness (AMS): When ascending to high altitudes, increased pressure in the skull caused by too much blood being pumped to the brain can lead to headaches, insomnia, dizziness, loss of appetite and nausea. Developing a cough and/or severe shortness of breath can indicate that the condition has worsened to high altitude pulmonary edema (HAPE), a leaking of fluid into the lungs. If an individual develops AMS and loses coordination and/or lapses into periods of unconsciousness, this is an indication of high altitude cerebral edema (HACE), fluid leaking into the brain. Both HAPE and HACE are potentially fatal, and immediate steps should be taken to immediately move the individual to a lower altitude and to seek medical attention. The best steps to acclimatize to altitude and prevent AMS are the following:

1. Spend some time (at least 1 or 2 days) at an intermediate altitude before heading to the high altitude of the huts.

2. Drink lots of water leading up to your hut trip and during your hut trip.

3. Concentrate on eating foods high in carbohydrates, and avoid caffeine, salty foods and alcohol.

4. Check ahead of time with your doctor on using the prescription drug diamox to help speed up the acclimatization process.

Hypothermia: Hypothermia occurs when the body temperature falls to a dangerously low level. Hypothermia is a consequence of being in a cold environment and usually occurs when you are wet, tired, exposed to wind, dehydrated and have not eaten enough. Signs of hypothermia include lack of coordination, confusion and irritability, and shivering. Treating hypothermia should include taking off wet clothing, warming up, drinking (non-alcohol), and eating food, especially carbohydrate-rich foods. To help prevent hypothermia, avoid wearing cotton; use high-tech synthetic fibers, especially against the skin.

Injuries: Broken bones, bleeding, breathing problems and other types of injuries requiring attention can occur due to accidents both on the trail and in the hut. Treatment must be handled by your fellow hutgoers, so members of your group should be versed in basic first aid. No medical help will be available until the injured person is transported back down to civilization. Obviously, the best cure is prevention. When in the backcountry, away from medical help, it is extra important to be very careful, especially while skiing, around the hot stoves in the hut, while chopping wood, etc. Be prepared with a good first-aid kit, and know how to improvise with splints for broken bones and wraps for sprains. Blisters can also be a factor that cut short a hut trip, so be well prepared to both prevent blisters and deal with them.

18

Avalanches: The 10th Mountain suggested, standard routes to the huts and between the huts have been planned so as to avoid avalanche danger as much as is possible. On a few routes there may be minimal slide danger, but these will be noted in the guidebook and on the website. Anyone using routes other than the standard 10th Mountain routes to and between the huts, and anyone doing backcountry skiing from or near the huts, should be educated in recognizing potential avalanche hazards, how to avoid these hazards, and what to do in case a member or members of the group are caught in an avalanche.

Visit the 10th Mountain website for avalanche information along the routes to the huts, and visit the Colorado Avalanche Information Center website www.geosurvey.state.co.us/avalanche for up-to-date avalanche information for all of Colorado and for avalanche safety techniques. Click on Central Mountains and copy or memorize their avalanche safety reminders. Be aware of how to recognize and identify slopes that could possibly slide, using the factors of terrain, snowpack, and weather. The most critical factor is slope angle, any slope of 30° or more is a potential avalanche slope. If your group is going to wander off the standard routes, or ski backcountry slopes, be sure members of the group are educated in avalanche hazards and safety.

Emergency Evacuation: The group should be prepared to perform a self-rescue. This may include improvising a sled using the victim's skis, duct tape, and some ingenuity. If an evacuation is needed, it will be necessary to call 911 (if available) or contact the sheriff of the county in which the evacuation is to take place (Eagle County: 970-479-2200; Lake County: 719-486-1249; Pitkin County: 970-920-5310; Summit County: 970-668-8600). Cell phones may help, but they do not work at most of the huts. In some instances, moving to higher ground can help establish contact. If the cell phone does not work, one member of the group should ski out to the nearest telephone and call the sheriff. This person should have the GPS coordinates of the location of the victim, or a map marked with the location. Steps should be also taken to make a helicopter rescue possible if required. To possibly avoid paying the cost of an emergency evacuation, it is best to purchase a CORSAR card (see 10th Mountain website) before heading out on the trip.

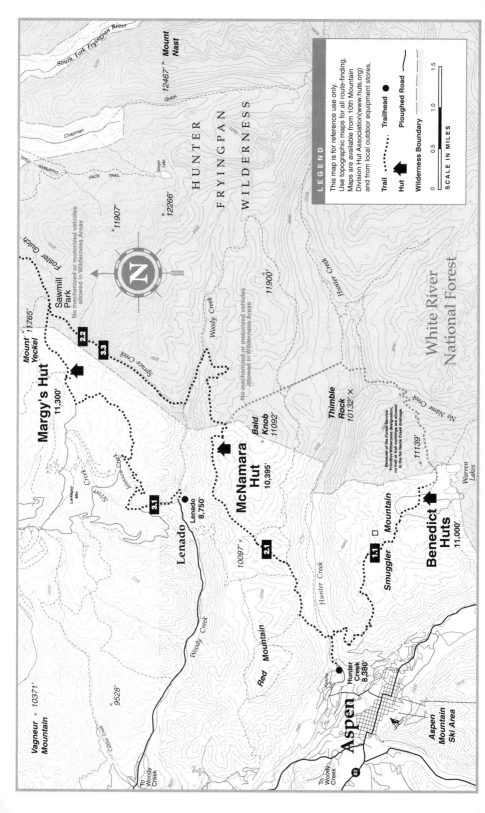

Chapter 1 • Benedict Huts

The Benedict Huts were named in honor of Fritz and Fabi Benedict, the spiritual parents of the 10th Mountain Hut System. It was Fritz, an architect and 10th Mountain Division veteran, who was the primary founder

Elevation: 11,000 feet
Coordinates: 13S0348341E, 4338121N
County: Pitkin
Access: Aspen

of the 10th Mountain Hut System. The Benedict Huts, consisting of the Fritz Hut which sleeps 10, and the Fabi Hut which sleeps 6 (and can be only booked by one group), are the most accessible huts to Aspen, and therefore are a popular trip for locals. The outhouse at these huts is without question the most infamous outhouse in the 10th Mountain Hut System. Where else is it possible to sit down and have two walls of glass exposing the outdoors to the seated one? The huts are not the usual log construction of most of the other huts in the system, but were constructed with well insulated panels, corrugated metal and barn siding, making them energy efficient and keeping down the costs.

No peak skiing exists around these huts; most just use the huts for relaxing or for cross-country ski tours. The Benedict Huts are mainly used as the sole destination for hutgoers, with no other huts conveniently located to make a hut-to-hut trip. However, it is possible to ski from the huts most of the way down to the trailhead and head up to McNamara Hut, but that would be a very long day.

1.1 Hunter Creek Trailhead to Benedict Huts

Difficulty: Intermediate (intermediate/advanced for skiers coming down)
Distance: 5.8 miles
Time: 6 hours up; 3-5 hours down
Text Map: p. 20
10th Mtn Map: Smuggler Mountain
USGS Map: Aspen
Elevation Gain: 2,620 feet

Notes: The trip to the huts, mostly via Smuggler Mountain Road, is wooded practically the entire way, but the early part does present some awesome views of Aspen, Aspen Mountain, and the entire Roaring Fork Valley. Parts of the first half of the route are quite steep, making it a very difficult return descent on skis, so many hutgoers choose snowshoes for this trip. The Hunter Creek Trailhead is the only designated access point.

Directions to Trailhead: In Aspen, by the Hotel Jerome at the intersection of Main St. (Hwy. 82) and Mill Street, go north on Mill Street. After crossing the bridge over the Roaring Fork River, bear left onto Red Mountain Road and continue up the hill to Hunter Creek Road (1.4 miles from Main Street with a sign for the Hunter Creek Trail parking lot). Go right for one-quarter mile and then left (just before the stone pillars) up to the parking lot (stay right at the private driveway). To get to the actual trailhead, walk down from the parking lot to Hunter Creek Road and go left through the stone pillars up the road .3 miles to the well-marked trailhead on the right (13S0343746E, 4340808N, 8,380 feet) just beyond a sharp switchback in the road. With a group it's best to drive up the road to the trailhead, drop everyone and their gear off, and then double back to park the car in the lot.

Route Description: From the trailhead put on your skins and traverse on the well-used trail to the Benedict Bridge crossing Hunter Creek. On the other side of the bridge a steady climb along the south side of Hunter Creek begins. Stay straight on this trail, avoiding private property, for about .5 miles until you come to the open area of Hunter Valley and a National Forest boundary sign. Continue straight along the right side of Hunter Creek, watching for a marked trail cutting up to the right. Many people simply angle up through the open area just beyond the sign. You will quickly intersect a road heading right (SW) and climbing via some steep switchbacks up the back side of Smuggler Mountain. The road tops out and switchbacks W at 9,000 feet at the Iowa Shaft, where a good view of the Hunter Valley to the north awaits you. Follow the road W as it traverses and then drops somewhat through the lodgepole pines to an intersection (13S0344216E, 4340478N, 8,870 feet) with the Smuggler Mountain Road.

The trail leaving the road into the woods about one-half mile before the huts.

Go left up the Smuggler Mountain Road as it traverses around the front side of the mountain with views over Aspen. At the intersection by the signed Smuggler Mountain open space (13S0344595E, 4340070N, 9,145 feet), stay right on the Smuggler Mountain Road as it continues to ascend quite steeply to 10,200 feet, where the grade begins to ease. At 10,500 feet a slight downhill takes you past an open park on your left, beyond which you continue on a gradual ascent. In another one-half mile, as you reach an elongated clearing extending to your right, watch for the trail leaving the road into the woods on the left (13S0347958E, 4338885N, 10,650 feet). From this point the narrow trail climbs steeply through the woods for the last .6 miles to the huts, located on a wooded knoll.

Reverse Route: From the back of the huts, go along the ridge about 100 feet and turn left (NW) onto the marked trail. A steep downhill traversing descent on the narrow trail takes you to the intersection of the Smuggler Mountain Road by the open marsh area. Continue straight on the road into the trees for a gradual downhill. Cross the tip of the open meadow in another half mile. A gradual uphill for a quarter mile leads to first a gradual descent, and then a steep winding descent on the road to the Smuggler Mountain open space area where you bear left to go around the front side of Smuggler Mountain.

As you curve to the right and come to a road intersection (13S0344216E, 4340478N, 8,870 feet), go right on a slight uphill. (Note: there may be two tracked roads to the right at this point. Take the second, watching for the blue diamond markers; the other is private.) Follow the road on a climbing traverse through the pines to an overlook over Hunter Valley at the Iowa Shaft. From here the road bends left and heads in a northerly direction, dropping into Hunter Valley via a series of steep switchbacks. As you come off the last steep section, watch for the left to take you through the open area of Hunter Valley toward Hunter Creek.

Just before Hunter Creek you will pick up the Hunter Creek Trail going left (W) along the south side of the creek as it drops for the last half mile to the Benedict Bridge, crosses the bridge and traverses to the paved road where you take off your skis and walk down the road .3 miles to the Hunter Creek Trailhead parking area.

The infamous glass-walled outhouse.

24

Chapter 2 • McNamara Hut

McNamara, one of the two original huts of the 10th Mountain Hut System built in 1982, is the closest hut to Aspen. This hut and Margy's Hut were built by funds contributed by Robert McNamara,

Elevation: 10,395 feet
Coordinates: 13S0349914E, 4344094N
County: Pitkin
Access: Aspen

former Secretary of Defense, as a memorial to his wife Margy. The only trailhead access to McNamara Hut is from the Hunter Creek Trailhead, and the amount of skiing and touring in the vicinity of the hut is somewhat limited. The most popular activity from the hut is the trip to nearby 11,092-foot Bald Knob for a great tour to a summit with spectacular 360° vistas of the entire region, and some good turns coming down. The 8.2-mile route between the McNamara and Margy's huts is a wonderful, wooded route that can present a navigational challenge after a fresh snow, or early in the season when the route is usually untracked.

2.1 Hunter Creek Trailhead to McNamara Hut

Difficulty: Intermediate
Distance: 5.7 miles
Time: 5-7 hours up; 4 hours down
Text Map: p. 20
10th Mtn Map: Smuggler Mountain
USGS Map: Aspen, Thimble Rock
Elevation Gain: 2,015 feet

Notes: The only trailhead to the McNamara Hut lies just up the hill from downtown Aspen. The route is well traveled, so direction finding is usually not difficult. The climb is steady and the views of Aspen and the Elk Mountain Range are worth taking in.

Directions to Trailhead: In Aspen, by the Hotel Jerome at the intersection of Main St. (Hwy. 82) and Mill Street, go north on Mill Street. After crossing the bridge over the Roaring Fork River, bear left onto Red Mountain Road and continue up the hill to Hunter Creek Road (1.4 miles from Main Street with a sign for the Hunter Creek Trail Parking Lot). Go right for a quarter mile and then left (just before the stone pillars) up to the parking lot (stay right at the private driveway). To get to the actual trailhead, walk down from the parking lot to Hunter Creek Road and go left through the stone pillars up the road .3 miles to the well-marked trailhead on the right (13S0343746E, 4340808N, 8,380 feet) just beyond a sharp switchback in the road. With a group it's best to drive up the road to the trailhead, drop everyone and their gear off, and then double back to park the car in the lot.

Route Description: Start with your skins on at the trailhead, you'll need them soon. Follow the trail, somewhat level, for a couple of hundred yards to the Benedict Bridge over Hunter Creek. The trail then begins an upward climb along the right side of the creek. At about one-half mile stay straight as the trail crosses a private road. In about 200 yards you will enter an open area at the National Forest Boundary. Stay straight along the right side of the creek for about 5 minutes to a trail going left over the creek, crossing the 10th Mountain Bridge. Cross the bridge and angle up left about 150 yards to a roadbed. Follow this road up (avoid side trails) towards a wooden fence and stay right, continuing on a steady uphill climb heading NE above Hunter Valley.

In a little over a mile, at a signed intersection at Lenado Gulch, bear right toward Van Horn Park and the McNamara Hut. You will pass through a small clearing and a gate, take a short climb through the aspen and enter the spacious expanse of Van Horn Park at about 9,500 feet. The trail heads NE along the left side of Van Horn Park, sometimes cutting through trees at the edge of the park. At the far end of Upper Van Horn Park, the trail comes to a saddle (13S0347653E, 4343708N, 9,920 feet) and angles right up into the trees. Follow a narrow road cut a little over 1.5 miles through the conifers, first NE,

then in an easterly direction toward the hut, staying high above the Woody Creek drainage which is off to your left. Shortly before the hut, the trail goes over the top of the ridge and curves right. In 100 yards you come to the hut boundary sign, enter a small clearing, and go left along the ridge to the hut.

The McNamara kitchen.

Reverse Route: From the front of the hut, go about 100 feet through the clearing and turn right (N) to follow the marked trail that soon goes over the slight ridge and curves to the east, following a road cut high above the Woody Creek drainage in the trees. Just under 2 miles from the hut, the route exits the trees onto a slight open saddle at 9,920 feet. From here the trail continues SW along the right edge of Upper Van Horn Park, and then drops through a few trees into Lower Van Horn Park. On exiting the park at 9,500 feet, the trail descends through a few aspen, passes through a gate and small clearing, and continues descending on a road cut traversing above Hunter Valley, first W, then turning S to drop to the valley floor. When packed, this entire downhill can be quite fast, so control your speed. On reaching the wooden fence and private property, go left (E) to cross Hunter Creek over the 10th Mountain Bridge. Take a right on the other side of the bridge and follow the trail along Hunter Creek as it descends somewhat steeply for almost a mile to the trailhead at the road. Take your skis off and head down the road the last .3 miles to the trailhead.

2.2 McNamara Hut to Margy's Hut

Difficulty: Intermediate/advanced
Distance: 8.2 miles
Time: 7-9 hours
Text Map: p. 20
10ᵗʰ Mtn Map: Smuggler Mountain
USGS Map: Thimble Rock, Meredith
Elevation Gain: 1,885 feet; loss: 980 feet

Notes: This is one of the more interesting hut-to-hut routes in the trees. The route drops to the Woody Creek drainage and then ascends the Spruce Creek drainage most of the way to the hut. Most of this trail is in wilderness, so watch carefully for trail blazes to stay on the route. Extreme care should be taken when reaching the gully that drops north toward Woody Creek, so as to stay on the trail above the gully on the east side. The old route through the gulch is dangerous and very obstacle prone. Save some strength for the last 4.5 uphill miles to Margy's. Watch for bank sluffs along the steep north side of the Woody Creek drainage and for potential avalanche activity on the steep slopes along Spruce Creek in the half mile above the intersection with Woody Creek during periods of high avalanche danger.

Route Description: From the porch of the hut, head SW (on the trail toward Bald Knob) about 200 feet, to a clearing where you take a sharp left (E) over a small creek to pick up the blazed trail cut heading east on the other side of the creek/gulch. Do not drop into the gulch between the hut and this trail. In less than ½ mile the marked trail loops around a small drainage, climbs slightly on the other side, and then contours at around 10,400 feet. At a clearing with the remains of a couple of old log cabins (13S0351524E, 4344463N) go left uphill on the other side of the cabins. After traversing about 10 minutes, you come to a very small clearing at the top of a gully with a trail going to the left (13S0351864E, 4344297N, 10,200 feet; watch for a blaze on the trail).

Take a left, and from this point watch your map and compass very closely, as trail finding becomes more difficult. About 100 feet down the trail from the clearing bear right to cross the creek and start angling up the right side of the gully (toward NE). Do not follow the old trail down the gully. The trail stays on the right (E) above the gully heading N, then rounding the ridge at about 10,100 feet and heading E along a trail cut which drops toward Woody Creek. At 9,910 feet the trail cuts

28

across Woody Creek (13S0352333E, 4344753N) and cuts back left on the other side, taking an easy climb NW for about 200 yards to the Woody Creek Trail (13S0352232E, 4344858N, 9,930 feet).

Follow the Woody Creek Trail on a steep, narrow downhill high above Woody Creek for .9 miles to the intersection with the Spruce Creek Trail at 9,440 feet. Go right on the Spruce Creek Trail about 200 yards to a crossing of Spruce Creek, put on your skins, and begin the 3.1-mile steady climb along the west side of Spruce Creek. When you come to the open area, Sawmill Park, on your right (13S0353972E, 4349128N, 11,030 feet), watch for a trail going left (W) at the beginning of the park. Contour first W, then SW, following the trail marked by blazes, for 1.3 miles to the wilderness boundary, go up a slight ridge and drop down through a small clearing SW to the hut.

The trail at Sawmill Park heading off into the woods towards Margy's Hut.

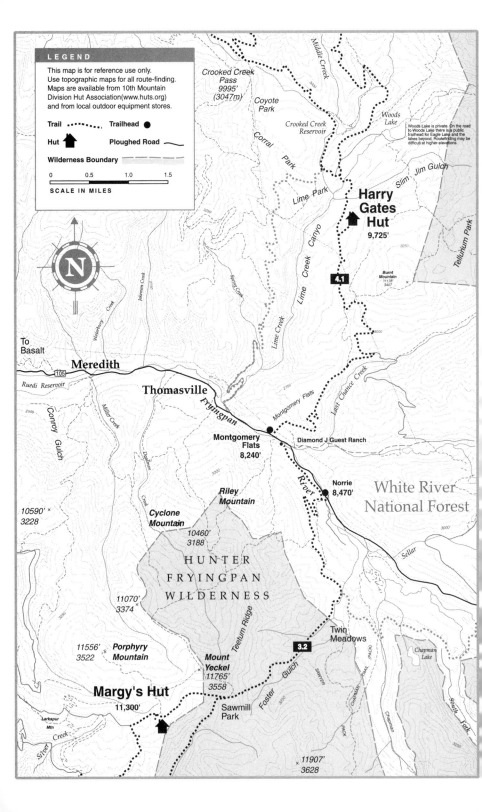

N

Crooked Creek
Pass
9995'
(3047m)

Coyote
Park

Middle Creek

Crooked Creek
Reservoir

Woods
Lake

Woods Lake is private. On the road
to Woods Lake there is a public
trailhead for Eagle Lake and the
lakes beyond. Routefinding may be
difficult at higher elevations.

Corral   Park

Lime Park

Harry
Gates
Hut
9,725'

Slim Jim Gulch

Tellurium Park

Spring Creek

Lime Creek

Lime Creek Canyon

4.1

Burnt
Mountain
11178'
3407

To
Basalt

Waterbury Creek

Ivanman Creek

Meredith

105

Ruedi Reservoir

Miller Creek

Conroy Gulch

Thomasville

Fryingpan

Montgomery Flats

Last Chance Creek

Diamond J Guest Ranch

River

Norrie
8,470'

White River
National Forest

Montgomery
Flats
8,240'

Dibman Creek

Riley
Mountain

Cyclone
Mountain

10460'
3188

10590' ×
3228

HUNTER
FRYINGPAN
WILDERNESS

11070'
3374 ×

Teetum Ridge

Sellar

11556'
3522 ×

Porphyry
Mountain

Mount
Yeckel
11765'
3558 ×

Foster Gulch

Twin
Meadows

3.2

Sawyer

PACK

CHAPMAN Trail

Chapman
Lake

Margy's Hut
11,300'

Larkspur
Mtn

Sawmill
Park

PACK

Chapman

South Fork

Silver Creek

× 11907'
3628

Chapter 3 • Margy's Hut

Margy's Hut was one of the first two huts of the 10th Mountain huts and was built in 1982. The hut is located at the top of a hillside on the flank of Mount Yeckel with spectacular

Elevation: 11,300 feet
Coordinates: 13S0352198E, 4348725N
County: Pitkin
Access: Lenado, Fryingpan Valley

views out to the Elk Mountain Range to the south. The hillside in front of the hut offers good skiing, especially with new snow (the south-facing slope can sometimes be crusty or a little bit heavy). The hut's most popular playground is nearby Mount Yeckel, which has some good gentle slopes for beginner and intermediate telemarkers, and for tours.

The direct route to the hut is from Lenado via Johnson Creek, but the longer route from the Norrie Trailhead in the Fryingpan Valley is also a pleasant, though somewhat more difficult, ski-in. The ski-through to the McNamara Hut covers a beautiful wilderness route, requiring some navigation skills. Skiing through to the Harry Gates Hut is a long trip and should only be attempted by the fittest skiers ready for a long day. It's best to break up the trip between these huts with an overnight stay at the Diamond J Guest Ranch, where you can soak in their hot tub.

3.1 Lenado Trailhead to Margy's Hut

Difficulty: Intermediate
Distance: 6.3 miles (from the parking lot)
Time: 5-6 hours up, 4 hours down
Text Map: p. 20
10th Mtn Map: Smuggler Mountain
USGS Map: Aspen, Meredith
Elevation Gain: 2,550 feet

Notes: This route is the shortest and most direct to Margy's Hut. The obvious road cuts and trails are easy to follow, but it does involve steady climbing most of the way. A flat stretch in the middle provides good lunch spots and some spectacular views of the Elk Mountain Range. Several potential avalanche slopes and gullies exist along the Woody Creek and Silver Creek drainages when the avalanche danger is high. A potential avalanche slope in the Johnson Creek drainage is crossed, but under normal conditions it is usually not a threat.

Directions to Trailhead: From Highway 82 turn north at the Woody Creek Canyon exit (Smith Way), about 7 miles west of Aspen. Just after crossing the Roaring Fork River at .3 miles, take a left onto Upper River Road (CR 17) and go 1.5 miles to a sharp right onto the Woody Creek Road (CR 18) toward Lenado. Follow the narrow winding road (4-wheel drive preferred but not necessary), and at 8 miles you enter the town of Lenado. At 9 miles you reach the trailhead (13S0348835E, 4345412N, 8,750 feet) at the small bridge over the creek. Drop off your gear and passengers and backtrack .4 miles to the 10th Mountain chained winter parking lot (8,640 feet) to park the car. The combo on the 10th Mountain lock on the chain is the same as the combo for the Margy's Hut.

Route Description: Follow the road over the bridge and continue on the gradual uphill climb for about a mile to where the road cuts back sharply to the left (13S0348325E, 4346625N, 9,080 feet). On the right, a trail goes up steeply and is marked by a sign on a post "Johnson Creek Trail # 2184". Put on skins, if you haven't done so already, and head up the steep trail along Silver Creek, crossing over the creek and then crossing back at just under 9,300 feet to head E up the left side of Johnson Creek. After crossing Johnson Creek in another half mile, traverse around to the right and enjoy the first view of the Elk Mountain Range.

You then take some long uphill traverses until you come to a wide road cut at 10,540 feet (13S0349813E, 4347081N). Turn right onto the road and continue through a relatively flat section with more great views of the Elk Mountain Range to the south. In a little over a mile the route steepens and winds for another mile to one last uphill, where you crest at a saddle at 11,255 feet (13S0351358E, 4348434N). About 150 feet on the other side of the saddle head right (E) on a road for one-half mile to an open area. Take the trail going right (E) to Margy's through some trees. The route may also be tracked out from the summer parking area through the woods. From here it's just a couple hundred yards to the hut which sits at the top of an open hillside.

The author's wife along the trail at a viewpoint for the Elk Mountain Range.

Reverse Route: Head up the short hill behind Margy's Hut and ski NW through the field about 100 yards to the road where you go left (W) for ½ mile. Go left to the low saddle at 11,255 feet just off the road and follow the road cut on the other side down 2.3 miles to where the Johnson Creek Trail drops off to the left at 10,540 feet (just down the trail should be a sign "Johnson Creek Trail # 2184"). Follow the trail as it traverses and winds down along the Johnson Creek drainage, crossing the creek at 9,600 feet and then crossing Silver Creek at 9,300 feet. A steep downhill takes you to the wide road where you turn left for the last mile to the trailhead.

3.2 Norrie Trailhead to Margy's Hut

Difficulty: Intermediate
Distance: 7.6 miles
Time: 7-9 hours up, 5-6 hours down
Text Map: p. 30
10ᵗʰ Mtn Map: Mount Yeckel
USGS Map: Meredith
Elevation Gain: 2,890 feet; loss: 60 feet

Notes: This route to Margy's, longer and harder than the route from Lenado, is certainly more scenic. The initial section on the road has great views of the Fryingpan Valley. The route continues through the spacious Twin Meadows with a backdrop of mountain peaks, and ends with an adventurous climb through stately conifers to Sawmill Park and Margy's Hut. Almost half of the route passes through wilderness and is therefore only marked with tree blazes. Especially close attention must be paid to route finding in the Twin Meadows area, and from Sawmill Park to the hut. The only potential avalanche hazard is on the steep slope above (west of) the road about a mile from the trailhead. Overnight lodging can be found at the Diamond J Guest Ranch or Double Diamond Ranch near the trailhead.

Directions to Trailhead: Take Highway 82 to Basalt (20 miles NW of Aspen) and turn at the light into downtown Basalt on the north side of the highway. Follow the Fryingpan River Road east from Two Rivers Road in Basalt for 28.0 miles (to the 28-mile marker) and turn right at the sign for Norrie Colony. Go across the bridge and straight up a short hill to a plowed parking area on the right (13S0356989E, 4354742N, 8,470 feet). Do not block the private driveway.

Route Description: Across from the parking area a distinct road cut takes off (to the right of a big rock) to the SW, gradually climbing up the side of the valley, heading SSE after two long switchbacks. Snowmobiles occasionally use this road, so it may be tracked out. At 9,320 feet watch carefully for a narrow 10ᵗʰ Mountain marked trail (the Aspen-Norrie Trail) going uphill off to the right through the trees (13S0357098E, 4352477N). (Note that about 150 yards before this trail on the right is a road cut going through a gate on the right that some people mistakenly take). If possible, save your skins for after Twin Meadows. Follow this trail up through the woods for a little under a half mile into the open area, Twin Meadows. Watch your map and compass here as the trail through the meadow isn't always obvious. Go straight ahead in a SSW direction, following a berm and staying along the right edge of the meadow at about the same elevation. Bear right around the clump of trees you first saw ahead on entering the meadow, and stay to the right of Deeds Creek. Since you are now in wilderness, the route will be marked by blazes on the trees along the edge of the open area. At the far end of the open area the trail cut heads into the trees to the right of the creek, and is evident as it continues right of the creek.

When the trail crosses over Deeds Creek it goes SW uphill on the other side of the creek. Put your skins on here if you haven't already done so. The trail, well marked by blazes, climbs steeply uphill through the trees along Foster Gulch. At 10,000 feet the trail passes through the upper edge of a large clearing, continuing to climb steeply. At 10,400 feet you will be going through several clearings which require close watching for the tree blazes marking the trail leaving these areas. Beyond these clearings the trail climbs even more steeply through a shallow gully.

At just over 11,000 feet the trail turns NW into the trees and leads you through a fairly level spot into Sawmill Park. Angle to the right across Sawmill Park and follow the right edge on a slight descent to the lower right (W) edge of the park where the trail intersects (13S0353972E, 4349128N, 11,030 feet) with the Spruce  Creek Trail and the route going right (NW) through the woods to Margy's. Go right (NW), contour first W, then SW, following the trail marked by blazes, for 1.3 miles to the wilderness boundary, go up a slight ridge and drop down through a small clearing SW to the hut.

Reverse Route: From Margy's Hut go NE up the hill behind the outhouse. At the wilderness boundary watch for the blazed trail (no more blue diamonds). Contour first NE then E for 1.3 miles, gradually dropping to Sawmill Park (13S0353972E, 4349128N, 11,030 feet). The first part will take cautious route finding unless a trail is already broken. Go left (ENE) through the park to the far east end where the marked trail leaves the park. Follow the blazes as the trail drops steeply. This section can be somewhat treacherous under difficult snow conditions, otherwise many good turns can be made on the route down. After crossing Deeds Creek the trail levels off and follows the left (W) side of Twin Meadows, entering the woods near a large rock and heading through the trees down to the wide road cut. Follow the road for about 2.5 miles on a gradual descent down into the Fryingpan Valley to the Norrie Trailhead and parking area.

3.3 Margy's Hut to McNamara Hut

Difficulty: Intermediate
Distance: 8.2 miles
Time: 6-8 hours
Text Map: p. 20
10ᵗʰ Mtn Map: Smuggler Mountain
USGS Map: Meredith, Thimble Rock
Elevation Gain: 980 feet; loss: 1,885 feet

Notes: This beautiful mostly wooded route, the oldest hut-to-hut route, lies almost entirely within wilderness boundaries, so tree blazes mark the way instead of the blue diamonds. In the early season, before the route is tracked out, this may make trail finding somewhat more difficult, so be prepared! Going down Spruce Creek can be a little testy in bad snow conditions, but a real joy with fresh snow. Pay close attention to the turns on and off the Woody Creek Trail. Skins won't be needed until you reach the Woody Creek Trail. Watch for potential avalanche activity on the steep slopes along Spruce Creek in the half mile before the intersection with Woody Creek during periods of high avalanche danger. Bank sluffs along the steep north side of the Woody Creek drainage are also possible after heavy snows.

Route Description: From Margy's Hut go NE up the hill behind the outhouse. At the wilderness boundary watch for the blazed trail (no more blue diamonds). Contour, first NE then E for 1.3 miles, gradually dropping to Sawmill Park (13S0353972E, 4349128N, 11,030 feet). The first part will take cautious route finding unless a trail is already broken. About 10 yards before entering the park follow the trail to the right as it drops down along the right side of Spruce Creek. Care should be taken where the trail passes through a boulder field. Just over 3 miles from Sawmill Park the trail crosses over Spruce Creek to the left side, and in another 200 yards comes to the signed intersection with the Woody

Creek Trail above the confluence of Spruce Creek and Woody Creek. Put on your skins and go left, starting with a steep climb up the Woody Creek Trail. The trail, marked by tree blazes, climbs fairly steadily above Woody Creek. At the top of a short rise, about 200 feet past an old Margy's Hut sign on a tree, (13S0352232E, 4344858N, 9,930 feet), go right on a blazed trail angling SE toward the creek. Cross the creek and continue following the blazed trail as it angles up to the right for almost one-half mile above the Woody Creek drainage. At 10,100 feet the trail rounds a ridge and traverses S above a gulch. At 10,200 feet, at a very small clearing at the head of the gulch, the trail takes a sharp right, following a traverse towards McNamara Hut. In about .4 miles the trail goes around the ruins of a couple of old cabins in a small clearing, bearing right on the other side. The trail cut with blazes is easy to follow, and at 1.4 miles beyond the cabin ruins comes to a clearing where you go right over a small creek and head NE for the last 100 yards along the ridge to the hut.

3.4 Margy's Hut to Harry Gates Hut

Difficulty: Intermediate/advanced
Distance: 16 miles
Time: 10-12 hours
Text Map: p. 30
10th Mtn Map: Mount Yeckel
USGS Map: Meredith, Crooked Creek Pass
Elevation Gain: 2,040 feet; loss: 3,615 feet

Notes: This obviously is not meant to be done in a day, except for the very hardiest hutgoers. The Diamond J Guest Ranch is a good overnight stopping point for those wishing to do this route between the two huts.

Route Description: From Margy's Hut follow reverse route 3.2 to the Norrie Trailhead. At the last switchback before the trailhead take the trail off to the left (usually snowmobile packed) to the Diamond J Guest Ranch. From here you will have to go .3 miles left on the Fryingpan Road to the Montgomery Flats Trailhead on the other side of the road. Follow route 4.1 to the Harry Gates Hut.

The Diamond J lodge.

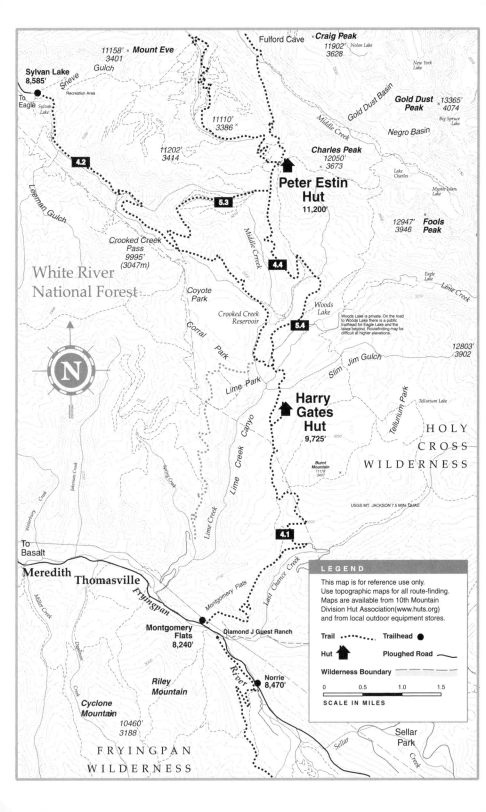

Chapter 4 • Harry Gates Hut

The Harry Gates Hut is at the lowest elevation of any of the 10th Mountain huts, making it an easy hut to get to for novice hut skiers. The hut is quite spacious and sits on a small knoll with spectacular views of Avalanche Peak and the Avalanche Ridge. For

Elevation: 9,725 feet
Coordinates: 13S0358004E, 4362456N
County: Eagle
Access: Basalt and the Fryingpan Valley; Eagle

those interested in exploring beyond the hut, Slim Jim Gulch is a good tour, and Burnt Mountain is a worthy objective for the adventurous interested in good turns in the glades and for a relatively easy peak climb. A few experienced ski mountaineers have been known to go all the way to the summit of Avalanche Peak and back in a day, although this is not recommended.

The primary and easiest access to the hut is from the Montgomery Flats Trailhead in the Fryingpan Valley. Some hutgoers coming from the east take the much longer route to the hut from Sylvan Lake, accessed through Eagle, often to do a loop that includes the Peter Estin Hut.

4.1 Montgomery Flats Trailhead to Harry Gates Hut

Difficulty: Novice/Intermediate
Distance: 6.8 miles
Time: 5-6 hours up, 4-5 hours down
Text Map: pp. 30, 38
10ᵗʰ Mtn Map: Burnt Mountain, Mount Yeckel
USGS Map: Meredith, Crooked Creek Pass
Elevation Gain: 2,005 feet, loss: 520 feet

Notes: This route, mostly following roads, is one of the easier routes to a hut, but still gains quite a bit of elevation. The way is highlighted by some great views of the Elk Mountain Range. The power lines, which occasionally detract from the views, are useful in pinpointing your location on the map. Lodging in the Fryingpan Valley is available at the rustic Diamond J Guest Ranch near the trailhead, or at the nearby Double Diamond Ranch.

Directions to Trailhead: From the 4-way stop sign in Basalt at the intersection with Two Rivers Road , follow the Fryingpan River Road about 26.5 miles to a driveway on the left (street number 26501), .3 miles before the Diamond J Guest Ranch. Turn up the driveway and park in the plowed 10ᵗʰ Mountain lot (13S0355152E, 4356706N, 8,240 feet) without blocking the driveway.

Route Description: From the parking lot go up the driveway about 100 yards to where trail takes off to the right just before a metal gate. Follow the blue diamonds through sagebrush and boulders along the power line, then up along a fence line to a traverse into the aspen. In about .6 miles from the trailhead go left on a road cut angling uphill through the aspen. At 9,200 feet, 1.6 miles from the trailhead, after a steady uphill has taken you into the conifer, the trail flattens and you bear to the left onto Montgomery Flats. After an easy 1.5 miles along Montgomery Flats, the trail intersects with Burnt Mountain Road (13S0358240E, 4358815N, 9,560 feet). Go left on the road as it continues on a gradual uphill, crossing under the power line 4 times. Just after the 4ᵗʰ crossing, take your skins off for the gradual 2-mile downhill to the vicinity of the hut. Just before the fence line across the road, where the road starts to rise (9,600 feet), bear right into the open meadow (you may need skins) for the last ¼ mile up the hill to the hut. Or, stay on the road just past the open meadow, and turn right onto a road cut for a gentler ascent to the hut.

Lunch on the road to the Harry Gates Hut.

Reverse Route: From the hut ski SW down the hill a quarter mile to the road and go left up the road. The 2-mile gradual uphill on the road doesn't require skins if you can wax, or if you have a fish scale base on your skis. From the summit at the first power line crossing, it is an easy 1.5 miles downhill on the road to the trail intersection (13S0358240E, 4358815N, 9,560 feet) on the right which you take WSW toward Montgomery Flats. After the 1.5 miles on the marked trail through the Flats, the downhill starts with some fairly steep narrow sections that require caution when snow conditions aren't the best. In a mile, watch for the marked trail off to the right which takes you the last .6 miles back through the aspen, sagebrush and boulders, under the power line and to the driveway, where you go left to the parking lot.

4.2 Sylvan Lake Trailhead to Harry Gates Hut

Difficulty: Intermediate
Distance: 10.8 miles
Time: 9-10 hours up; 6-8 hours down
Text Map: p. 38
10ᵗʰ Mtn Map: Burnt Mountain
USGS Map: Crooked Creek Pass
Elevation Gain: 1,940 feet; loss: 800 feet

Notes: This long route to the Harry Gates Hut is not the most efficient way in, most access the hut from the Montgomery Flats Trailhead in the Fryingpan Valley. However, hutgoers coming from I-70 and the Denver area can save on driving by using this trailhead. It can also be used in conjunction with a trip to the Peter Estin Hut, creating a long, but scenic loop from Sylvan Lake to the two huts. Navigation is relatively easy, since the entire route follows roads which are usually packed out by snowmobiles. However, care must be taken in Lime Park where poor visibility and intersecting routes can cause confusion. Skins are not needed on this route to the hut if you have skis with fish scales or a good wax.

Directions to Trailhead: From I-70 take the Eagle Exit #147 south for .2 miles to a right onto Highway 6 just over the Eagle River bridge. Take the first left off Highway 6 onto Capitol and go .8 miles to Brush Creek Road. Turn left onto Brush Creek Road, and follow Brush Creek Road (signed at the turns) for 10.2 miles to a "Y". Take the right fork (West Brush Creek Road) towards Sylvan Lake. Drive 5 miles to parking at the Sylvan Lake Trailhead (13S0350955E, 4371632N, 8,585 feet) at the state park. There are a few parking spaces right at the end of the plowed road.

Route Description: Continue straight up the West Brush Creek road cut as it gently rises above Sylvan Lake and Brush Creek. At the first road fork past Sylvan Lake stay left going uphill on the West Brush Creek Road towards Crooked Creek Pass. Continue climbing as you switchback up to some good views over the valley and surrounding mountains. At 5.3 miles from the trailhead you reach Crooked Creek Pass (13S0354965E, 4367126N, 10,045 feet). Continue straight on Road 400 as it gradually drops into Crooked Creek Park, crosses Crooked Creek and goes along the west side of Crooked Creek Reservoir. It then follows the Little Lime Creek drainage down to a signed intersection (13S0357129E, 4364103N, 9,320 feet), with Road 507 going left. Turn left (SE) on Road 507 and follow it .4 miles ESE to the intersection with Burnt Mountain Road #506 (13S0357653E, 4363849N, 9,320 feet) by a fence line, gate and sign. Turn right (S) on Burnt Mountain Road and follow it S to a crossing (13S0357780E, 4363621N, 9,215 feet) of Lime Creek at the entrance to Lime Creek Canyon.

Continue on Burnt Mountain Road as it slowly climbs up into the trees at first, and then through open area and more trees for about 1.2 miles to an intersection (13S0357568E, 4362271N, 9,580 feet) with a road cut on the left and a sign pointing to the Gates Hut. Follow the road cut left through a gate as it gradually climbs  below a ridge and then circles up to the right onto the ridge where the hut is located.

Reverse Route: From the Harry Gates Hut, ski W about 80 feet and turn right onto a road cut which you follow on a gradual downhill as it cuts back to Burnt Mountain Road. Take a right on Burnt Mountain Road and follow it down about 1.2 miles to the Lime Creek crossing at the entrance to Lime Creek Canyon. Continue up right for about 200 yards to the intersection of roads 506 and 507 (13S0357653E, 4363849N, 9,320 feet) by a fence line, gate and sign. Go left up the hill and follow Road 507 in a WNW direction. Continue on this heading which will take you along the right side of a small drainage (Little Lime Creek) to an intersection with Road 400 (13S0357129E, 4364103N, 9,320 feet) marked by a sign showing Thomasville to the left and Eagle to the right. This is the road you will be following to Crooked Creek Pass and the Sylvan Lake Trailhead. Go right towards Eagle, continue along the left side of Crooked Creek Reservoir, beyond which the road crosses Crooked Creek to the north side. A steady, easy climb takes you to Crooked Creek Pass (13S0354965E, 4367126N, 10,045 feet). Continue on the road on a gradual downhill for another 5.3 miles to the Sylvan Lake Trailhead.

4.3 Harry Gates Hut to Margy's Hut

Difficulty: Intermediate (intermediate/advanced if done in one day)
Distance: 16 miles
Time: 12-14 hours
Text Map: p. 30
10th Mtn Map: Mount Yeckel
USGS Map: Meredith, Crooked Creek Pass
Elevation Gain: 3,615 feet; loss: 2,040 feet

Notes: This obviously is not meant to be done in a day, except for the very hardiest hutgoers. The Diamond J Guest Ranch in the Fryingpan Valley (reservations must be made through the Diamond J, not 10th Mountain) is a good overnight stopping point for those wishing to do this route between the two huts.

Route Description: Follow reverse route 4.1 to the Montgomery Flats Trailhead, walk .3 miles up (left) the Fryingpan Road to the Diamond J Guest Ranch and take the 1.4 mile track (usually snowmobile packed) to the Norrie Trailhead. Follow route 3.2 to Margy's Hut.

4.4 Harry Gates Hut to Peter Estin Hut

Difficulty: Intermediate
Distance: 7 miles
Time: 6-9 hours
Text Map: p. 38
10th Mtn Map: Burnt Mountain
USGS Map: Crooked Creek Pass
Elevation Gain: 2,115 feet; loss: 640 feet

Notes: This route between the Harry Gates Hut and Peter Estin Hut via the Lime Ridge Trail is fairly direct and quite scenic. It avoids snowmobile traffic by using just trail, except for the initial portion of the route. The section along the top of Lime Ridge is one of the most interesting and scenic of any of the 10th Mountain hut routes. The route is fairly well marked, except for the portion through Lime Park which requires close attention to map and compass, especially in poor visibility conditions. Much of the route is uphill, making this a physically demanding trip, so the trip in the opposite direction is easier if you have a choice.

Route Description: From the hut, ski W about 80 feet and turn right onto a road cut which you follow on a gradual downhill as it cuts back to Burnt Mountain Road. Take a right on Burnt Mountain Road and follow it down about 1.2 miles to the Lime Creek crossing at the entrance to Lime Creek Canyon. Continue up right for about 200 yards to the intersection of roads 506 and 507 (13S0357653E, 4363849N, 9,320 feet) by a fence line, gate and sign. From this point get out your compass and continue through the open area on a slightly rising traverse on a N heading. (Note: You are no longer following a road at this point and this section is not marked).

At 9,480 feet (13S0357708E, 4364393N) you will enter the trees and follow a marked 10th Mountain trail that curves around to the NE to gain the summit of the narrow Lime Ridge. Follow the crest of the ridge NE on a gradual uphill to 9,800 feet. Here the trail drops N off the ridge on an easy downhill that circles through the trees to a crossing of Lime Creek at 9,680 feet (13S0359054E, 4366264N). Continue NW, soon passing to the right of a pond in a depression in an open area. Continue NW along the right side of a small drainage.

At 9,750 feet (13S0358470E, 4366873N) you will cross the creek on your left at a well-marked crossing and take a sharp left (S) on the other side to continue on a climbing traverse through the trees on the side of the ridge. As the trail reaches the south side of the ridge at 9,900 feet it turns sharply NW and climbs the ridge through an open area (watch your compass). It continues through more trees and along the right side of another open area, soon switchbacking up the ridge on a well-marked trail for almost 2 miles.

At 10,860 feet the trail breaks out of the trees into an open area on top of the ridge. Continue straight on a N heading along the ridge above the head of Spine Creek, watching your compass closely to head N then NNE as the area opens up. Watch for the occasional blue diamond as the trail goes along the right side of the ridge toward the hut. After one last uphill through an open area the trail enters the 10th Mountain summer parking area (13S0357884E, 4369555N, 11,130 feet), from where the marked trail goes out the left side the last short distance E to the Peter Estin Hut (13S0358096E, 4369681N), somewhat hidden at the edge of the trees.

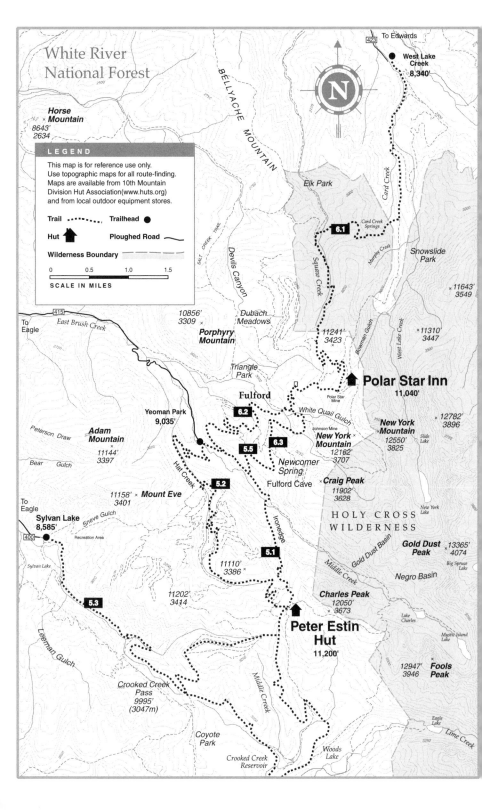

Chapter 5 • Peter Estin Hut

The Peter Estin Hut is a perennial favorite for hut skiers for many reasons. The hut sits on a forested ridge looking out over Lime Park onto the Elk Mountain Range to the south. All types of skiing and touring are available

Elevation: 11,200 feet
Coordinates: 13S0358096E, 4369681N
County: Eagle
Access: Eagle

from the hut, especially touring and skiing Charles Ridge, which includes Charles Peak (12,050 feet) and Fools Peak (12,947 feet). Nearby Prospect Peak (11,845 feet) offers easier skiing for those looking for a short climb and some turns.

Access to the hut is from either Yeoman Park or Sylvan Lake. After a fresh snow, the last 5-6 miles to these trailheads may not be plowed for a couple of days, so 4-wheel drive and snow tires is a must under these conditions. Yeoman Park is the most efficient access, and therefore the most popular trailhead for the hut. Most skiers prefer to go up the steep Ironedge Trail to get to the hut from Yeoman Park, and to return via the easier Hat Creek Trail.

5.1 Yeoman Park Trailhead to Peter Estin Hut via Ironedge Trail

Difficulty: Intermediate up, advanced down
Distance: 4.4 miles
Time: 5-6 hours up, 4 hours down
Text Map: p. 46
10ᵗʰ Mtn Map: New York Mountain
USGS Map: Crooked Creek Pass, Fulford
Elevation Gain: 2,115 feet

Notes: The Ironedge Trail from Yeoman Park is the most efficient access to the Peter Estin Hut and is almost always used as the ascent route to the hut. The trail is a snowmobile-free, beautiful steep climb through the woods, but can be a nightmare for less experienced skiers coming down, especially under poor snow conditions. So, for most skiers, the recommended descent route is via Hat Creek (5.2), a longer but quick descent from the hut to Yeoman Park. A couple of potential avalanche slopes exist on the steep slopes of the Ironedge Trail in the first mile above the Fulford Cave Campground, but under normal conditions are usually not a threat.

Directions to Trailhead: From I-70 take the Eagle Exit #147 south for .2 miles to a right onto Highway 6 just over the Eagle River bridge. Take the first left off Highway 6 onto Capitol and go .8 miles to Brush Creek Road. Turn left onto Brush Creek Road, and follow Brush Creek Road (signed at the turns) for 10.2 miles to a "Y". Take the left fork (East Brush Creek Road) 6.0 miles to Yeoman Park, turn right over the bridge and park in the parking area (13S0355695E, 4374040N, 9,085

feet). This road will usually require 4-wheel drive and snow tires under snowy conditions.

Route Description: From the parking area walk back over the bridge (N) and turn right onto the East Brush Creek Road. At

.4 miles the road takes a sharp switchback to the left. Do not switchback left on the road, but continue straight on the road cut toward Fulford Cave. At 1.0 miles stay straight again as the Newcomer Spring Trail goes up to the left toward the Polar Star Inn.

At the Fulford Cave Campground go left around a small lake, following the signs to Ironedge Trail #1873 (do not take the uphill trail cut for Trail #1899 at the lake). This is a good place to put on your skins for what lies ahead. Just past the lake, you will come to some private residences on the left, beyond which the trail starts its ascent. You soon cross to the west side of the creek and continue on a switchbacking, steep ascent of over 1,000 vertical feet. The route eases somewhat as you come to some open areas near the top. Be aware that several road cuts and occasional false tracks veer from the trail in this area; watch closely for the 10th Mountain marked trail.

At 10,820 feet (13S0357679E, 4370348N) you come to the Ironedge Saddle where the Hat Creek drainage and trail drops off to the west and the trail to the hut heads SSE. Remember this junction for your return trip, as it is easy to drop into the wrong drainage. Also, avoid following tracks on a road cut, but stay on the blue diamond marked trail SSE for the most direct route to the hut. You will quickly enter a small gully which you follow up to the final marked SE ascent through scattered trees to the hut. Watch your compass and altimeter closely.

Reverse Route: From the front porch, go right and ski NW into the trees on the marked trail. You can make some turns as you drop NW, and then down a small gully on the right. Beware of tracks going in other directions. On leaving the gully you wind down through some trees and soon come to the Ironedge Saddle at 10,820 feet (13S0357679E, 4370348N).

From here the Ironedge Trail drops down to the right (N), while the route down Hat Creek goes left (W) and down the other side of the saddle through an open area. Stay right on the Ironedge Trail as it drops, and drops, and drops via switchbacks along the west wall of the drainage to the East Brush Creek crossing at 9,400 feet, then passes some private residences, and circles around the right of the small lake at Fulford Cave Campground. From here follow the road cut along the north edge of Yeoman Park as it slowly descends NW for 1.4 miles to the left turn over the bridge for the parking area.

5.2 Yeoman Park Trailhead to Peter Estin Hut via Hat Creek Trail

Difficulty: Intermediate
Distance: 7.3 miles
Time: 6-8 hours up, 4-6 hours down
Text Map: p.46
10th Mtn Map: New York Mountain
USGS Map: Crooked Creek Pass, Fulford
Elevation Gain: 2,115 feet

Notes: This trail is a long and tedious route to get to the Peter Estin Hut, so most take the more scenic and efficient Ironedge Trail up. However, the trail down Hat Creek is much easier than the Ironedge descent, and is preferred as the descent route by most less experienced skiers.

Directions to Trailhead: From I-70 take the Eagle Exit #147 south for .2 miles to a right onto Highway 6 just over the Eagle River bridge. Take the first left off Highway 6 onto Capitol and go .8 miles to Brush Creek Road. Turn left onto Brush Creek Road, and follow Brush Creek Road (signed at the turns) for 10.2 miles to a "Y". Take the left fork (East Brush Creek Road) 6.0 miles to Yeoman Park, turn right over the bridge and park in the parking area (13S0355695E, 4374040N, 9,085 feet). This road will usually require 4-wheel drive and snow tires under snowy conditions.

At the Yeoman Park Trailhead.

Route Description: From the parking area go S on the road toward the camping loops. In about 100 yards after crossing the creek, watch for the road cut on the right heading up into the trees (SE) just before the camping loops. This is the Hat Creek Road which you will be following to the hut. After switchbacking NW and rising above Yeoman Park for about a mile, the road switchbacks to the SE for the slow ascent to the hut. In another mile, at 9,540 feet at a road junction, stay left on Road

416. Do not follow the West Hat Creek Road (#436) which goes right over the creek. Just beyond this junction, where you enter an open area, follow the switchback up through the open area and watch for the road cut as it exits the SE end of the clearing. From here on the road cut is quite evident, taking several switchbacks from 9,800 feet to 10,200 feet as it follows the left side of the drainage.

As you come to the head of the drainage just below 10,800 feet, take care to head east to the Ironedge Saddle at 10,820 feet (13S0357679E, 4370348N), avoiding the road cut up on your right, and take your bearings. Here the Ironedge Trail goes left (N) down into the drainage on your left, and your trail to the hut goes right (SSE) toward the Peter Estin Hut. Remember this junction for your return trip, as it is easy to drop into the wrong drainage. Also, avoid following tracks on a road cut, but stay on the marked trail which heads up SSE for the most efficient route to the hut. You will quickly enter a small gully which you ascend to the final marked SE ascent through scattered trees to the hut. Watch your compass and altimeter closely.

Reverse Route: From the front porch, go right and ski NW into the trees on the marked trail. You can make some turns as you drop NW, and then down a small gully on the right. Beware of tracks going in other directions. On leaving the gully you wind down through some trees and soon come to the Ironedge Saddle at 10,820 feet (13S0357679E, 4370348N). From here the Ironedge Trail drops down to the right (N), while the route down Hat Creek goes left (W) and down the other side of the saddle through an open area. Stay along the right side of this open area for the gradual descent into the Hat Creek drainage, picking up a road cut that will continue on the right (E) side of Hat Creek for the next 5½ miles.

The road soon traverses high above the creek and then at 10,200 feet begins a slow descent back toward the creek via several long switchbacks. At 9,700 feet, watch the route carefully as it switchbacks down through a large clearing (a chance to make a few turns) toward the creek and then goes right, soon coming to a road junction at 9,540 feet which goes left across the creek. Stay straight along the right side of Hat Creek. In about 1 mile a sharp switchback to the right takes you down the final easy descent into Yeoman Park and the parking area for the trailhead.

5.3 Sylvan Lake Trailhead to Peter Estin Hut

Difficulty: Intermediate
Distance: 9.5 miles
Time: 8-10 hours up; 5-8 hours down
Text Map: p. 38
10th Mtn Map: Burnt Mountain
USGS Map: Crooked Creek Pass
Elevation Gain: 2,695 feet; loss: 80 feet

Notes: This route goes to the Peter Estin Hut via Crooked Creek Pass. Because of its length, this is not the route of choice to get to this hut. Most prefer one of the shorter, more efficient routes from the Yeoman Park Trailhead. However, for those who wish to visit both the Peter Estin and Harry Gates huts in one trip, a wonderful loop can be made from the Sylvan Lake Trailhead. Most of the route to the Peter Estin Hut follows a gently ascending road, much of it usually packed by snowmobiles. Only the last mile is on trail, where there can be a few navigational difficulties if care is not taken. The entire route, except for maybe the last few hundred yards, can be done using skis with fish scales or wax. Save the skins for the last little climb.

Directions to Trailhead: From I-70 take the Eagle Exit #147 south for .2 miles to a right onto Highway 6 just over the Eagle River bridge. Take the first left off Highway 6 onto Capitol and go .8 miles to Brush Creek Road. Turn left onto Brush Creek Road, and follow Brush Creek Road (signed at the turns) for 10.2 miles to a "Y". Take the right fork (West Brush Creek Road) towards Sylvan Lake. Drive 5 miles to parking at the state park at the Sylvan Lake Trailhead (13S0350955E, 4371632N, 8,585 feet). There are a few parking spaces right at the end of the plowed road.

Route Description: Continue straight up the West Brush Creek road cut as it gently rises above Sylvan Lake and Brush Creek. At the first road fork past Sylvan Lake stay left going uphill on the West Brush Creek Road towards Crooked Creek Pass. Continue climbing as you switchback up to some good views over the valley and surrounding mountains. At 5.3 miles from the trailhead you reach Crooked Creek Pass (13S0354965E, 4367126N, 10,045 feet), about 200 feet past the Red Mountain Trail going off to the right. At the pass, go left (NW) just before the fence line going up the hill, where a sign indicates the route to the Peter Estin Hut. You will be following the Hat Creek Road #416 for the next 3 miles. At 10,760 feet the road drops very slightly to a nondescript saddle with an open space on the left and trees on the right.

In about 200-300 yards past the saddle the road takes a sharp switchback left (13S0357288E, 4368694N, 10,770 feet) as it crosses Spine Creek. Just over the creek take a right and continue through the partly open area E (watch your compass carefully) up the hill for several hundred yards to the top of the top of a ridge. If you miss the trail markings, just stay due E to reach the ridge top. Just over the top of the ridge (13S0357549E, 4368582N, 10,900 feet), take a left (N), watching for blue diamonds as you get into the trees, and continue in a NNE direction as the trail goes along the right side of the ridge toward the hut. After an uphill requiring skins, you will reach the 10th Mountain summer parking area (13S0357884E, 4369555N, 11,130 feet) from where the marked trail goes out the left side the last 150 yards E to the hut, somewhat hidden at the edge of the trees.

Reverse Route: Head W from the hut for about 150 yards to the 10th Mountain summer parking area. (Take care not to drop down on the marked trail heading N toward the Ironedge Saddle). Head S on the marked trail from the parking area, staying along the left side of the ridge and watching for the occasional blue diamond. About .7 miles from the hut, the trail drops down through an open area to the right (13S0357549E, 4368582N, 10,900 feet) at the head of the Spine Creek drainage. This intersection may not be well marked, just follow the drainage down, heading W for several hundred yards to where the drainage crosses the Hat Creek Road (13S0357288E, 4368694N, 10,770 feet). Go left (W) on the road on a gradual downhill and continue following the road for a little over 3 miles as it gradually descends to Crooked Creek Pass. At the pass, take a right (WNW) on the West Brush Creek Road for the final 5.3-mile gradual descent along the wide road cut to the Sylvan Lake Trailhead.

5.4 Peter Estin Hut to Harry Gates Hut

Difficulty: Intermediate
Distance: 7 miles
Time: 5-7 hours
Text Map: p. 38
10th Mtn Map: Burnt Mountain
USGS Map: Crooked Creek Pass
Elevation Gain: 640 feet; loss: 2,115 feet

Notes: This route between the Peter Estin Hut and Harry Gates Hut using the Lime Ridge Trail is fairly direct and quite scenic, following a trail for all but the last 1.8 miles. The tour along the top of Lime Ridge is one of the most interesting sections of any of the hut-to-hut routes. The route is fairly well marked, except for the portion through Lime Park, which requires close attention to map and compass, especially in poor visibility. Much of the route is downhill; under good snow conditions it can be a fairly quick enjoyable trip, under poor conditions a bit of a challenge on the steep downhills. The entire route can be done without using skins if you have skis with fish scales or a good wax.

Route Description: Head W from the hut for about 150 yards to the 10th Mountain summer parking area. (Take care not to drop down on the marked trail heading N toward the Ironedge Saddle). Head S on the marked trail from the parking area, staying along the left side of the ridge and watching for the occasional blue diamond. About .7 miles from the hut, where the trail drops down through an open area to the right (13S0357549E, 4368582N, 10,900 feet) at the head of the Spine Creek drainage, stay straight (S) along the ridge to enter the woods on the 10th Mountain marked trail. The well-marked trail switchbacks in the trees down the ridge fairly steeply, leveling off somewhat as it enters some open areas at 10,200 feet. Continue heading in a SE direction, initially staying along the left edge of the clearings and watching for the occasional blue diamonds in the trees.

After passing through the last clearing the trail drops into a hillside of aspen and takes a sharp left turn, as it traverses N on the steep hillside in the trees, dropping down to a creek drainage and crossing the creek at 9,750 feet (13S0358470E, 4366873N). On the other side of the creek the trail takes a sharp right and continues just above the creek, heading SE toward Little Lime Creek. As you come into an open area with a pond in a depression on the right, keep going straight (SE) across the open area to the marked trail in the woods that climbs over a very slight rise and drops down to cross Little Lime Creek at 9,680 feet (13S0359054E, 4366264N).

After the crossing, stay straight on a little uphill (no skins necessary) and continue to follow the well-marked trail in the trees fairly level to one last easy climb to the top of Lime Ridge between Woods Lake and Crooked Creek Reservoir. Follow the crest of this narrow, wooded ridge with great views off to each side. On breaking out of the trees at 9,480 feet (13S0357708E, 4364393N) into the open area of Lime Park, take a compass reading and head directly S on a slowly dropping traverse toward the entrance to Lime Creek Canyon ahead. Watch for the intersection at 9,320 feet (13S0357653E, 4363849N) of the route with the Burnt Mountain Road (Road 506) by a fence line, sign and gate. Continue S on Burnt Mountain Road to a crossing (13S0357780E, 436362N, 9,215 feet) of Lime Creek at the entrance to Lime Creek Canyon.

Continue on Burnt Mountain Road as it slowly climbs up into the trees at first, and then through some open area and more trees for about 1.2 miles to an intersection (13S0357568E, 4362271N, 9,580 feet) with a road cut on the left and a sign pointing to the Gates Hut. Follow the road cut left through a gate as it gradually climbs below a ridge and then circles up to the right onto the ridge where the hut is located.

5.5 Peter Estin Hut to Polar Star Inn

Difficulty: Intermediate/advanced
Distance: 8.2 miles
Time: 7-9 hours
Text Map: p. 46
10th Mtn Map: New York Mountain
USGS Map: Crooked Creek Pass, Fulford
Elevation Gain: 1,860 feet; loss: 2,020 feet

Notes: As described here, the route goes down the Ironedge Trail to East Brush Creek Road and ascends the Newcomer Spring route to the Polar Star Inn. This is the most efficient route, but requires advanced skiing skills for the descent of the Ironedge Trail, especially under less than ideal snow conditions. An easier, although much longer route would be to descend Hat Creek (5.2) from the Peter Estin Hut and ascend the Fulford Road or Newcomer Spring route (6.2) from Yeoman Park to the Polar Star Inn, a total distance of 13.5 miles. Either route requires careful navigation in the Fulford area and above.

Route Description: From the front porch, go right and ski NW into the trees on the marked trail. You can make some turns as you drop NW, and then down a small gully on the right. Beware of tracks going in other directions. On leaving the gully you wind down through some trees and soon come to the Ironedge Saddle at 10,820 feet (13S0357679E, 4370348N). From here the Ironedge Trail drops down to the right (N), while the route down Hat Creek goes left (W) and down the other side of the saddle through an open area. Stay right on the Ironedge Trail as it drops, and drops, and drops via switchbacks along the west wall of the drainage to the East Brush Creek crossing at 9,400 feet, then passes some private residences, and circles around the right of the small lake at Fulford Cave Campground. From here follow the road cut along the north edge of Yeoman Park as it slowly descends NW for .4 miles to the Newcomer Spring Trail which goes up on the right (13S0356946E, 4373207N, 9,300 feet).

Put your skins on and climb this steady ascent route through the aspen trees, watching carefully for 10th Mountain trail markers. At 9,980 feet the trail flattens out, crosses a road cut, and continues on a northerly, fairly level traverse with spectacular views of the surrounding mountains to the west. After a sharp bend to the right, the route continues on a traverse high above Fulford, heading first SE, then NE as it drops to cross Nolan Creek. The trail then climbs slightly around a knoll and descends to cross White Quail Gulch in Upper Town past a cabin ruin. From here the trail goes west a short distance, passing through a few aspen and emerging into an open area with a cabin ruin about 100 feet up to the right. Head up through the clearing to the left of the cabin. Watch your compass and map very closely in this area.

A couple of hundred feet above the cabin, get off the road cut and follow the marked 10th Mountain trail to the right into a few trees. The trail switchbacks in the open area and then heads up to the left (NW) into the conifers where it becomes easier to follow. A steep climb through aspen and some conifers finally tops out at 10,540 feet where you take a right onto a jeep trail. Follow the jeep trail N a short distance until you come to a sharp switchback going back up to the right (SE). Follow this marked trail uphill on a steady climb through the trees.

As the trail levels off at 10,840 feet you come to an intersection with a road cut going off to the right (13S0358937E, 4375814N). Stay straight/ left through a couple of trees (watch for trail markings) for about 100 yards to where the road stays left and the marked 10th Mountain trail goes up to the right (13S0359066E, 4375849N, 10,870 feet). Go right as the trail cut starts curving up easterly and then northeasterly towards the Polar Star Inn for the last ½ mile.

Chapter 6 • Polar Star Inn

The Polar Star Inn which sleeps 17, and the adjacent Carl's Cabin which sleeps 6, are both privately owned, but are booked by the 10th Mountain Division Hut Association. Carl's Cabin is small and cozy with one double bedroom downstairs, and two double bedrooms upstairs. The tall Polar Star Inn has two levels of outside decks, and inside is very similar to the other 10th

Mountain huts, except that the lights are run by gas, and running water can be gotten from an outside hydrant. New York Mountain, located just to the southeast of the Inn makes a wonderful winter playground, offering great

Elevation: 11,040
Coordinates: 13S0359602E, 4375975N
County: Eagle
Access: Eagle, Edwards

touring and a winter peak ascent, as well as skiing for intermediate and advanced level skiers. The Yeoman Park routes to the Polar Star are the most direct routes to the hut, with the Newcomer Spring route being

more scenic and quieter than the Fulford Road, which is used by snowmobiles. The longer West Lake Creek route through the wilderness is one of the most pleasant hut access routes in the entire system.

Carl's Cabin.

6.1 West Lake Creek Trailhead to Polar Star Inn

Difficulty: Intermediate/advanced
Distance: 7 miles
Time: 8-9 hours up, 5-6 hours down
Text Map: p. 46
10ᵗʰ Mtn Map: New York Mountain
USGS Map: Grouse Mountain, Fulford
Elevation Gain: 3,100 feet; loss: 400 feet

Notes: The West Lake Creek Trailhead is normally used only for ski-throughs between the I-70 corridor and the Fryingpan Valley or Aspen, and is not very heavily traveled. A shorter easier route to the Polar Star Inn is from Yeoman Park via the Fulford Road or Newcomer Spring Trail. However, over half of the West Lake Creek route is in wilderness, helping make this one of the more scenic ski routes to a hut. Route finding in the wilderness, especially early in the season or after a heavy snow, will require a lot of attention to detail on the part of the hut skier.

Directions to Trailhead: Exit I-70 at exit 163 (Edwards) about 13 miles west of Vail. Go south on the exit road past a Rest Area and over Eagle River to Highway 6 (.5 miles). Turn right and go .7 miles to Lake Creek Road and turn left. Drive 1.9 miles up Lake Creek Road to a right onto West Lake Creek Road. Go 2.8 miles to a parking area where the road makes a switchback to the left. A sign indicates West Lake Trail. When the snow isn't too deep, and if you have 4-wheel drive, you can drive up the road (Road 423) out of the parking area .2 miles up the West Lake Creek drainage to the trailhead (13S0361484E, 4383510N, 8,340 feet). Otherwise walk/ski up. A map and porta-john are located at the trailhead.

Route Description: From the trailhead ski the road which immediately crosses West Lake Creek and ascends along the right (W) side. In ¾ mile the road crosses back over the creek and continues through the trees, bordered by private property. The road continues its ascent on the east side of the drainage above Card Creek. At a little over 2 miles from the trailhead watch closely for Card Creek Trail going off to the right at 9,445 feet (13S0361482E, 4380714N). There may be a sign on a tree here indicating "No Garbage Service, Please Pack it Out". Follow the marked trail (often not packed out) as it descends past Card Creek Spring and then enters the wilderness (now marked by tree blazes), heading east, using switchbacks to ascend the ridge beyond the spring.

Watch your map and compass closely to gain Card Creek Saddle at 10,000 feet. From the saddle head W through the small open area into the woods to pick up a dropping traverse which takes you SW into the Squaw Creek drainage, where you cross Squaw Creek at 9,840 feet.

The trail then continues to gradually climb up the Squaw Creek drainage, making several creek crossings, the last at 10,200 feet to take you up to a sharp right (S) at 10,250 feet. The trail reaches a saddle at 10,630 feet, at the head of the drainage about 1.8 miles from the first Squaw Creek crossing. Go along the east side of the saddle, cross the wilderness boundary, and climb SE, following a road cut at 10,840 feet for a couple hundred yards. Watch closely for the trail cutting up into the woods from this road (13S0359371E, 4376520N, 10,950 feet) which is a shortcut back to the road above which takes you up toward the hut. You will come to the 10th Mountain summer parking area, a gate which you go through (or around), and the road cut that bends to the right and drops the last 200 feet to the hut.

Reverse Route: From the Polar Star Inn start slightly uphill past the outside woodpile (ENE) for about 200 feet to a small clear area and a road cut that bends to the north and down through a gate into the open area. Follow a road cut N on a gradual downhill toward a treed knob ahead. After a few hundred yards the road curves to the left; watch for the 10th Mountain marked trail going straight ahead into the conifers at this point. Take this shortcut back to the road. At a sharp switchback in the road to the left, the trail again goes off to the right in the trees.

In about a quarter mile, as the trail turns right, you enter the wilderness where the trail is marked by blazes, rather than blue diamonds. Stay along the east edge of the Squaw Creek Saddle and follow this beautiful steady downhill as the trail descends through the trees along the right (E) side of the Squaw Creek basin. At 10,250 feet the trail comes to a clearing where it goes sharply to the left and drops down to Squaw Creek, crosses over and follows Squaw Creek (with a couple of crossings) to 9,840 feet, where the trail crosses to the east side of the creek. The trail gradually curves NE to the Card Creek Saddle at 10,000 feet. From here it switchbacks down steeply E through the wilderness boundary to Card Creek Spring, beyond which a short uphill takes you onto a ridge which you follow down (N) to a road intersection at 9,445 feet. Go straight on this road as it descends (N), then drops and follows Card Creek and West Lake Creek to the trailhead.

6.2 Yeoman Park Trailhead to Polar Star Inn

Difficulty: Intermediate
Distance: 6.2 miles (via Fulford Road); 5.8 miles (via Newcomer Spring)
Time: 5-7 hours up, 3-5 hours down
Text Map: p. 46
10ᵗʰ Mtn Map: New York Mountain
USGS Map: Fulford, Crooked Creek Pass
Elevation Gain: 2,075 feet; loss: 120 feet

Notes: The Yeoman Park access is shorter and has less elevation gain than the West Lake Creek access, and is therefore the preferred trailhead for the Polar Star Inn. The route via the Fulford Road is often heavily traveled by snowmobiles, especially on the weekend. The Newcomer Spring route is not only more pleasant, but shorter. Both routes converge above Fulford for a steep ascent to the hut. Route finding in here can be tricky; close attention should be paid to the maps for this upper part of the route. For the return trip, the Newcomer Spring route involves a steep and sometimes treacherous downhill through the trees for the last mile down to the road. This can be wonderful for advanced skiers under good snow conditions, but can be a real challenge for less experienced skiers. Some route finding is also required on this route. Therefore, most less advanced skiers take the Fulford Road for the return trip.

Directions to Trailhead: From I-70 take the Eagle Exit #147 south for .2 miles to a right onto Highway 6 just over the Eagle River bridge. Take the first left off Highway 6 onto Capitol and go .8 miles to Brush Creek Road. Turn left onto Brush Creek Road, and follow Brush Creek Road (signed at the turns) for 10.2 miles to a "Y". Take the left fork (East Brush Creek Road) 6.0 miles to Yeoman Park, turn right over the bridge and park in the parking area (13S0355695E, 4374040N, 9,085 feet). This road will usually require 4-wheel drive and snow tires under snowy conditions.

Route Description: From the parking area walk back over the bridge (N) and turn right onto the East Brush Creek Road which you follow .4 miles to where the road takes a sharp switchback to the left. From here you can take either the Fulford Road route or the Newcomer Spring route to Fulford.

//Fulford Road Route// Take the switchback left (NW) and follow the wide Fulford road cut for 3.8 miles, as it climbs about 800 feet vertical and then drops slightly to Nolan Creek the last one-half mile. At Nolan Creek (signed), put on your skins, cross over the creek and go right on the Nolan Lake Trail towards Upper Town. Start heading uphill for a couple hundred yards and watch for the trail heading up through a clearing past the remains of an old log cabin.

//Newcomer Spring Route// Do not switchback left on the road, but continue straight on the road cut toward Fulford Cave. In .6 miles (13S0356946E, 4373207N, 9,300 feet) watch for the Newcomer Spring Trail going up to the left. Put your skins on and climb this steady ascent route through the aspen trees, watching carefully for 10th Mountain trail markers. At 9,980 feet the trail flattens out, crosses a road cut, and continues on a northerly, fairly level traverse with spectacular views of the surrounding mountains to the west. After a sharp bend to the right, the route continues on a traverse high above Fulford, heading first SE, then NE as

The author, taking a break to admire the view.

it drops to cross Nolan Creek. The trail then climbs slightly around a knoll and descends to cross White Quail Gulch in Upper Town past a cabin ruin. From here the trail goes west a short distance, passing through a few aspen and emerging into an open area with a cabin ruin about 100 feet up to the right. Head up through the clearing to the left of the cabin.

//Continuation for both the Fulford Road Route and the Newcomer Spring Route// A couple of hundred feet above the cabin, get off the road cut and follow the marked 10th Mountain trail to the right into a few trees. The trail switchbacks in the open area and then heads up to the left (NW) into the conifers where it becomes easier to follow. A steep climb through aspen and some conifers finally tops out at 10,540

In the kitchen of the Polar Star Inn.

feet where you take a right onto a jeep trail. Follow the jeep trail N a short distance until you come to a sharp switchback going back up to the right (SE). Follow this marked trail uphill on a steady climb through the trees. As it levels off at 10,840 feet you come to an intersection with a road cut going off to the right (13S0358937E, 4375814N). Be wary of tracks going to the right and stay straight/left through a couple of trees (watch for trail markings). In another 100 yards the road stays left and the marked 10th Mountain trail goes up to the right (13S0359066E, 4375849N, 10,870 feet). Go right as the trail cut starts curving up E and then NE towards the Polar Star for the last ½ mile.

Reverse Route: From the front deck of the Polar Star head SW through the open area on a gradual downhill. At the first road cut crossing continue straight on the trail, going downhill for a couple of more minutes to an intersection where a road cut goes off left (10,840 feet). Bear right on the marked 10th Mountain trail. Continue on a steady downhill for about 15 minutes to a road intersection where you take a sharp left (S) onto the wide road cut. Continue on a downhill for about 5 minutes; as the road takes a bend down to the right (10,540 feet) watch for the marked trail going off to the left through the aspen. Follow this trail on some good downhill curves through the aspen. When it levels somewhat you will be traversing across an open area, then back across to the right (W) and start dropping into Upper Town past the remains of an old cabin.

//Newcomer Spring Route// About 100 feet below the cabin ruin is the trail going off to the left (E) into the aspen. Follow this trail across the small White Quail Gulch, to the right of another ruin where an old sign indicates "Upper Town". The trail then starts on a gradual uphill, going

S on the other side of the gulch. It climbs slightly around a knoll, descends across Nolan Creek, and then curves right on a long traverse NW above the town of Fulford. When the high traverse takes a sharp bend to the left (S), you will have great views to the west of the surrounding mountains. Continue on a southerly traverse, cross a road and start dropping gradually, then much more steeply through the trees. Watch carefully for the marked trail, as it isn't always evident after fresh snow. After a mile of steep descent, the trail bottoms out at a road cut (13S0356946E, 4373207N, 9,300 feet). From here turn right for the last mile NW to the trailhead in Yeoman Park.

//Fulford Road Route// Continue downhill below the cabin toward the creek and watch for a trail heading to the right (W). Follow this trail W as it descends for about 200 yards to an intersection of roads at Nolan Creek. Go left (SW) to cross Nolan Creek and continue SW on the wide Fulford road cut as it first climbs slightly, then starts long traverses, slowly descending the 3.8 miles to East Brush Creek Road at Yeoman Park. Go right for the last .4 miles on the road to the Yeoman Park Trailhead.

6.3 Polar Star Inn to Peter Estin Hut

Difficulty: Intermediate
Distance: 8.2 miles
Time: 7-9 hours
Text Map: p. 46
10th Mtn Map: New York Mountain
USGS Map: Fulford, Crooked Creek Pass
Elevation Gain: 2,020 feet; loss: 1,860 feet

Notes: As described here, the route descends the Newcomer Spring route and ascends the Ironedge Trail. For an easier, but much longer route, the Fulford Road (6.2) and Hat Creek (5.2) routes can be used. Either way, this is a long hut-to-hut trip.

Route Description: From the front deck of the Polar Star head SW through the open area on a gradual downhill. At the first road cut crossing continue straight on the trail, going downhill for a couple of more minutes to an intersection where a road cut goes off left (10,840 feet). Bear right on the marked 10th Mountain trail. Continue on a steady downhill for about 15 minutes to a road intersection where you take a sharp left (S) onto the wide road cut. Continue on a downhill for about 5 minutes; as the road takes a bend down to the right (10,540 feet) watch for the marked trail going off to the left through the aspen. Follow this trail on some good downhill curves through the aspen. When it levels somewhat you will be traversing across an open area, then back across to the right (W) and start dropping into Upper Town past the remains of an old cabin.

About 100 feet below the cabin ruin is the trail going off to the left (E) into the aspen. Follow this trail across the small White Quail Gulch, to the right of another ruin where an old sign indicates "Upper Town". The trail then starts on a gradual uphill, going S on the other side of the gulch. It climbs slightly around a knoll, descends across Nolan Creek, and then curves right on a long traverse NW above the town of Fulford. When the high traverse takes a sharp bend to the left (S), you will have great views to the west of the surrounding mountains. Continue on a southerly traverse, cross a road and start dropping gradually, then much more steeply through the trees. Watch carefully for the marked trail, as it isn't always evident after fresh snow. After a mile of steep descent, the trail bottoms out at a road cut (13S0356946E, 4373207N, 9,300 feet). Go left (SE) here on the East Brush Creek Road toward Fulford Cave Campground.

At the Fulford Cave Campground go left around a small lake, following the signs to Ironedge Trail #1873 (do not take the uphill trail cut for trail #1899 at the lake). This is a good place to put on your skins for what lies ahead. Just past the lake, you will come to some private residences on the left, beyond which the trail starts its ascent. You soon cross to the west side of the creek and continue on a switchbacking, steep ascent of over 1,000 vertical feet. The route eases somewhat as you come to some open areas near the top. Be aware that several road cuts and occasional false tracks veer from the trail in this area; watch closely for the 10th Mountain marked trail.

At 10,820 feet you come to the Ironedge Saddle (13S0357679E, 4370348N) where the Hat Creek drainage and trail drops off to the west and the trail to the hut heads SSE. Avoid following tracks on a road cut, but stay on the blue diamond marked trail SSE for the most efficient route to the hut. You will quickly enter a small gully which you follow up to the final marked SE ascent through scattered trees to the Peter Estin Hut. Watch your compass and altimeter closely.

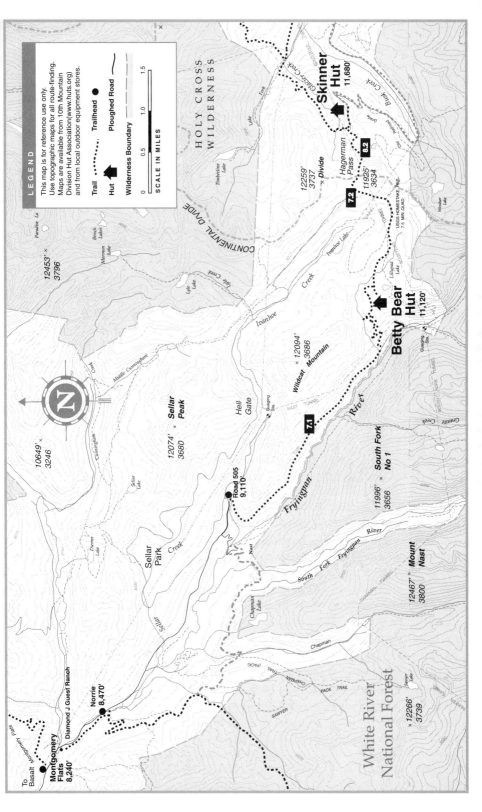

Chapter 7 • Betty Bear Hut

The Betty Bear Hut, located just west of Lily Pad Lake above the Fryingpan Valley, is a wonderful access point for touring open meadows, for ascending Hagerman Pass on the Continental Divide, and for skiing the slopes near the pass. The views of the Hunter-Fryingpan Wilderness from the upper level of the hut are spectacular, adding to the popularity of this destination.

Elevation: 11,120 feet
Coordinates: 13S0368549E, 4346304N
County: Pitkin
Access: Fryingpan Valley (Basalt)

The hut has a reversed floor plan from most of the other huts, with the sleeping quarters being on the lower level, and the kitchen and lounging area being upstairs. The Betty Bear Hut and the Skinner Hut, located on the other side of the Continental Divide, form an important link between the Aspen side of the Continental Divide and the Leadville/Vail side.

7.1 Road 505 Trailhead to Betty Bear Hut

Difficulty: Intermediate
Distance: 6.9 miles
Time: 6-8 hours up; 5 hours down
Text Map: p. 65
10ᵗʰ Mtn Map: Upper Fryingpan
USGS Map: Nast
Elevation Gain: 2,060 feet; loss: 80 feet

Notes: Most of the route to the Betty Bear follows the gentle grade of Road 505 with its spectacular views of the Fryingpan Valley. However, an extremely steep ascent of over 1,100 feet between Road 505 and the hut can cause difficulties for any level skier, especially on the return trip if the snow isn't the best, due to the southern exposure. Many skiers end up taking off their skis on part of the route and walking, especially on the descent, due to the extreme steepness, so beware! Others prefer to snowshoe up because of the difficulty in negotiating this section of trail. During periods of high avalanche danger, special care should be taken, as the route on the road crosses some avalanche runoff zones.

Directions to Trailhead: Take Highway 82 to Basalt, located halfway between Aspen and Glenwood Springs. From downtown Basalt take the Fryingpan Road (main street in Basalt) 26.6 miles to the Biglow Fork. Stay right on the Fryingpan Road for another 5.8 miles to Road 505 on the right, just before

At the Road 505 Trailhead.

a large curve to the left. Park in the plowed area (13S0363101E, 4351007N, 9,110 feet) at the beginning of Road 505.

Route Description: Follow Road 505 from the parking area for 4¾ miles as it very gradually ascends above the beautiful Fryingpan Valley. As you get toward the end of the valley watch carefully for a trail going up to the left from the road. The turnoff (13S0367290E, 4346459N, 9,995 feet) will be about 100 feet past the second of two natural stone gateways that alert you to its proximity, by the Lily Pad Creek crossing. From the road follow the very steep switchbacking marked trail up through the trees to the east of Lily Pad Creek. At 10,940 feet

(13S0368294E, 4346698N) you may have trouble finding the marked trail, as many hutgoers take a shortcut through the trees on a more direct line to the hut. To continue on the marked trail, stay on a NE direction (you will pick up blue diamonds just beyond this intersection) and then bend to the E through some clearings to an open area. Bear to the right (S) and watch for a trail intersection in the clearing marked by a sign post (13S0368654E, 4346488N). Follow the route W then SW on a slight descent for about 200 yards to the Betty Bear Hut.

Reverse Route: From the hut head NE up a short rise through the trees. In about 200 feet you may come to a shortcut heading W. To continue on the marked trail continue heading NE a little over 100 yards to a sign post and trail junction in a clearing. Head N and follow the marked route as it bends to the W and starts dropping (connecting with the short cut at 10,940 feet) down through several clearings and into the trees. A series of very steep switchbacks, where many have to use skins going down or take off their skis, leads you on a dizzying descent to Road 505 at 9,995 feet. Turn right and follow the road above the Fryingpan Valley as it gradually descends (with a few short rises) for 4¾ miles to the trailhead.

7.2 Betty Bear Hut to Skinner Hut

Difficulty: Advanced (due to navigational difficulties above timber line)
Distance: 4.4 miles
Time: 4-6 hours
Text Map: pp. 65, 70
10th Mtn Map: Upper Fryingpan
USGS Map: Nast, Homestake Reservoir
Elevation Gain: 925 feet; loss: 365 feet

Notes: This route over the Continental Divide can be one of the most enjoyable and scenic in the system (on a beautiful sunny day), or one of the most treacherous (under poor weather conditions). About half of the route is above timber line, making navigation difficult, and exposing the hutgoer to potential extreme weather conditions. Have a good map, compass, altimeter and be aware of changing weather conditions when making this trip. Some potential avalanche terrain will be encountered during high avalanche hazard periods, but can easily be avoided.

Route Description: From the Betty Bear Hut head N up the trail for about 200 yards on a slight uphill to the intersection (13S0368654E, 4346488N) marked by a sign post in an open area. Turn E toward Hagerman Pass. Watch the map and your compass closely as you head E then bend to the SE through the large open area bisected by Lily Pad Creek. Watch closely for the occasional blue diamonds, which eventually take you along the left (N) edge of the clearing. After bending to the E, you will head up into some trees and meet the road (13S0370503E, 4346155N, 11,450

On the trail near Hagerman Pass.

feet) that goes from Ivanhoe Lake to the Hagerman Tunnel. Follow the road E for three-quarters mile to where the road ends by the depression of the entrance to the Hagerman Tunnel on the right.

From here angle up the hill steeply beyond the tunnel entrance in a NNE direction for the steep climbing traverse toward the top of the Continental Divide. Watch your compass carefully, and watch for the occasional blue diamond, as you will be above timber line, and route finding could become a challenge. Keep on the steep uphill traverse. You will eventually come to a line of posts with blue diamonds to lead you NNE up the last section toward the power lines and Hagerman Pass. Do not cross under the power lines, stay to the right. You will come to a sign indicating Hagerman Pass (13S0372209E, 4347023N, 12,000 feet). Note that you will be above the low point of the pass.

Follow the Hagerman Pass Road down the other side, as it crosses a narrow spot at one point, overlooking Hagerman Lake situated down to the right. In just under a mile from the pass, watch carefully as the road takes a sharp turn to the left at 11,700 feet (13S0373184E, 4347067N), about 50 feet before some power lines. Follow the road NE on a descent for 100 yards to a ridge going up to the right (E). Take the marked trail up the ridge for .3 miles through the trees and small clearings to the hut.

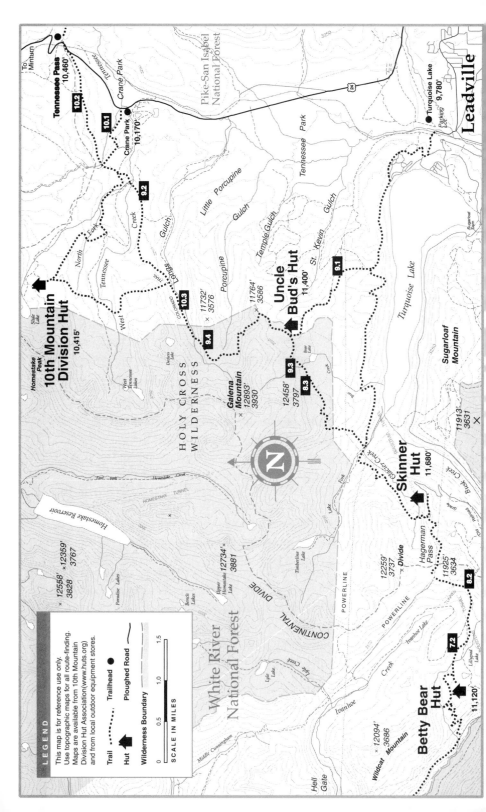

LEGEND

This map is for reference use only.
Use topographic maps for all route-finding.
Maps are available from 10th Mountain
Division Hut Association(www.huts.org)
and from local outdoor equipment stores.

Trail ·······   Trailhead ●

Hut ◢   Ploughed Road ━━

Wilderness Boundary ────

SCALE IN MILES

0   0.5   1.0   1.5

Tennessee Pass
10,460'
10.2
To Minturn
10.1
Crane Park
Crane Park
10,170'
Pike-San Isabel
National Forest
9.2
Turquoise Lake
9,780'
Parking
Leadville
24

10th Mountain
Division Hut
10,415'

Homestake
Peak
Slide
Lake

North Fork

West Tennessee Lakes

West

Tennessee Creek

Longs Gulch

Little Porcupine Gulch

Temple Gulch

St. Kevin Gulch

Tennessee Park

10.3
11732'
3576

9.4

Porcupine

COLORADO TRAIL

Uncle
Bud's Hut
11,400'

9.1

HOLY CROSS
WILDERNESS

Dickens Lake

Galena
Mountain
12893'
3930

11764'
3586

Bear
Lake

9.3

12458'
3797

8.3

Turquoise Lake

Sugarloaf
Mountain

3250

Sugartooth
Dam

N

Homestake Reservoir

× 12558' 12359'
3828 3767

12734' ×
3881

Upper
Homestake
Lake

Bench
Lakes

Paradise
Lakes

East Fork

Homestake Creek

CONTINENTAL DIVIDE

Fall Creek

Lyle
Lake

Lyle Creek

White River
National Forest

Timberline
Lake

Busk Creek

11913'
X 3631

Skinner
Hut
11,680'

Glacier Creek

12259'
3737
Divide

Hagerman
Pass

11925'
3634

POWERLINE

POWERLINE

Ivanhoe
Lake

Ivanhoe Lake

HOMESTAKE TUNNEL

8.2

7.2

Betty Bear
Hut
11,120'

Lillypad
Lake

Ivanhoe
Creek

Middle Cunningham

Hell
Gate

Wildcat
Mountain
× 12094'
3686

Chapter 8 • **Skinner Hut**

The Skinner Hut sits on a knoll just below the Continental Divide and overlooks the Holy Cross and Mount Massive Wilderness, with spectacular views of the many high peaks in the Mosquito Range east of Leadville. The

Elevation: 11,680 feet
Coordinates: 13S0373771E, 4347324N
County: Lake
Access: Leadville

Skinner Hut's one-story design with a stone exterior is unique in the 10th Mountain Division Hut System. The hut's isolated location at the top of a precipitous drop-off presents difficulties in access, but experienced hutgoers will certainly find a trip to the Skinner Hut to be a worthy adventure in high altitude navigation and conditioning. Getting to the Skinner Hut from a trailhead is probably the biggest adventure. The distance to the hut from the Turquoise Lake Trailhead on the Leadville side is 10.7 miles. From the Aspen side of the Continental Divide, the distance from the Road 505 Trailhead in the Fryingpan Valley to the Skinner Hut is 11 miles, which includes a trip over the Continental Divide. However, coming from the Fryingpan, most hutgoers stay overnight at the Betty Bear Hut, and then continue to the Skinner Hut the next day. The trip out from the Skinner Hut to Road 505 is quicker than the trip in, and is doable in a day under good weather conditions. The best skiing and touring from the Skinner Hut is on the Continental Divide in the Hagerman Pass area, but remember that this is high altitude above timber line, and weather is a major factor. The trip from the hut down the steep Glacier Creek route, which is part of the route to Uncle Bud's Hut and the Turquoise Lake Trailhead, is another challenge, but can be a wonderful adventure for the advanced skier under good snow conditions, which is the norm on this north-facing route.

8.1 Turquoise Lake Trailhead to Skinner Hut

Difficulty: Advanced
Distance: 10.7 miles
Time: 7-9 hours
Text Map: p. 70
10th Mtn Map: Continental Divide
USGS Map: Homestake Reservoir, Leadville North
Elevation Gain: 2,620 feet; loss: 720 feet

Notes: This long route goes along the easy-to-follow Turquoise Lake Road above the north side of Turquoise Lake and then rises over 1,600 feet along a very steep trail up the Glacier Creek drainage to the hut. This steep climb makes this an especially demanding route which requires good endurance. Expert skiing skills are definitely a must for the steep ascent down Glacier Creek on the return route. A potential avalanche slope in Glacier Creek below the Skinner Hut should be monitored during high hazard periods, but is normally not a problem.

Directions to Trailhead: From I-70 take Highway 24 or Highway 91 south to Leadville. At the north end of Leadville, turn W from Highway 24 onto Mountain View Drive (the light by the Safeway store). Go 2.9 miles to a T-intersection (CR9) and turn right. Go .5 miles (staying right at the first fork) to a large parking area (13S0384448E, 4346969N, 9,780 feet) on the right side of the road.

Route Description: Walk across the highway on the road (CR9) over the railroad tracks about 100 yards to the road closure and put on your skis. If you wax or have fish scales, skins won't be necessary for the first 7¾ miles. Follow the snow-covered road just over one-quarter mile to a T-intersection and turn right toward May Queen Campground. Continue following the main road, avoiding turns off to campgrounds and viewpoints, for another 3.2 miles on a gradual ascent.

As the climb seems to peak, watch for Forest Service Road 107 going off to the right (13S0380509E, 4348798N, 10,445 feet) toward Uncle Bud's Hut. Stay straight on FSR 104 (Turquoise Lake Road) to continue toward the Skinner Hut. Continue another 4.3 miles on the main road to the road intersection past the end of Turquoise Lake. Continue W on the road with a sign indicating the way to the Timberline Lake Trailhead. In 100 yards the road ends in a small open area (13S0375217E, 4349398N, 10,070 feet) with wooden fencing and trailhead signs.

From here follow the Colorado Trail uphill about 200 yards to the Timberline Lake Trailhead. Take a left (W) on the blue diamond marked trail at the "Closed to all Motor Vehicles" sign (do not follow the Timberline Lake Trail). Continue on a steady steep switchbacking and traversing ascent to a right turn in a small clearing at 10,640 feet. Continue SW. At the large clearing at 10,760 feet stay on a WSW bearing to enter a few trees on a marked trail that leads to the next clearing where you angle left to the far side of the clearing.

The Skinner outhouse.

From here you ascend up a small gully in the trees quite steeply, winding up to an open area at 11,160 feet at the foot of the steep rock faces below the hut. A gradual ascent through a couple of small open areas quickly leads to the final steep switchbacking ascent to the Hagerman Pass road at the head of the Glacier Creek drainage. Go E up the ridge on the left for the last .3 miles to the Skinner Hut.

Reverse Route: From the Skinner Hut ski W .3 miles down the ridge to the Hagerman Pass Road and look for the 10th Mountain marked trail on the right descending into the Glacier Creek drainage. The well-marked trail drops very steeply via switchbacks through the right side of the drainage. At 11,250 feet, the descent eases as you enter a large clearing. Stay right, heading E, and watch for the diamonds leading you down the creek drainage. After passing the steep rocky slope below the Skinner Hut, the trail again drops steeply down the gut of Glacier Creek, eventually coming out into a large clearing at 10,780 feet. Head ENE through the right side of the clearing, through about 150 feet of trees, and then into another large clearing. Head straight through the clearing to the far left end where the clearing curves left and the route exits the end of the clearing heading N.

From here the trail heads NE, dropping gently to a sharp left turn at 10,640 feet where you have to go left (NW) to avoid a precipitous drop. The trail traverses and switchbacks steeply down following blue diamonds and blazes marking the Colorado Trail to a junction with the Timberline Lake Trail at 10,110 feet (13S0375044E, 4349378N). Bear right, going downhill on the Colorado Trail for about 200 yards to a small open area (13S0375217E, 4349398N, 10,070 feet) with wooden fencing and trailhead signs. Bear right (ESE) on the road for about 100 yards to the Turquoise Lake Road junction right under the power lines. Follow the road left as it gradually ascends above the N side of Turquoise Lake, passing FSR 107 going left to Uncle Bud's Hut in 4.3 miles. Stay straight on the main road, avoiding turnoffs to viewpoints and campgrounds, for another 3 miles on a gradual descent to a left turn past Baby Doe Campground. Take the left for the last .3 miles to the trailhead.

8.2 Skinner Hut to Betty Bear Hut

Difficulty: Advanced (due to navigation above timber line at high
    altitudes)
Distance: 4.4 miles
Time: 4-5 hours
Text Map: pp. 65, 70
10th Mtn Map: Upper Fryingpan
USGS Map: Nast, Homestake Reservoir
Elevation Gain: 365 feet; loss: 925

Notes: This route can be one of the most enjoyable and scenic in the system (on a beautiful sunny day), or one of the most treacherous (under poor weather conditions). About half of the route is above timber line, making navigation difficult, and exposing the hutgoer to potential extreme weather conditions. Have a good map, compass, altimeter and be aware of changing weather conditions when making this trip. Some potential avalanche terrain will be encountered during high avalanche hazard periods, but can easily be avoided.

Route Description: From the Skinner Hut ski W for .3 miles down the ridge to the Hagerman Pass Road and go left (SSW) up the road for about 100 yards to the power lines where you follow the road to the right as it climbs 1 mile up to Hagerman Pass (13S0372209E, 4347023N, 12,000 feet). Watch your map and altimeter closely, as the road is not always obvious above timber line.

After you crest the pass, stay left of the power lines, and watch for the blue diamonds on poles above timber line, and then on trees. Follow the diamonds on a dropping traverse SSW (a good chance to do some turns, but don't drop below the route) down to the entrance to the Hagerman Tunnel, where the road from the tunnel to Ivanhoe Lake begins.

Follow the road for three-quarters mile W to a large open area where you leave the road at a turn at 11,450 feet (13S0370503E, 4346155N) and head left through a few trees. Watch your map and compass closely in the very large clearing as you follow a route initially close to the right side of the clearing, marked only very occasionally by a blue diamond. Head W then WNW through the middle of the clearing. Beyond the Lily Pad Lake clearing on the left, head back W to the left edge of the main clearing to a sign post (13S0368654E, 4346488N) where you are directed SW down a short downhill to the Betty Bear Hut.

Heading up Hagerman Pass from the Skinner Hut.

8.3 Skinner Hut to Uncle Bud's Hut

Difficulty: Advanced
Distance: 7 miles / 9.7 miles
Time: 8-10 hours
Text Map: p. 70
10ᵗʰ Mtn Map: Continental Divide
USGS Map: Homestake Reservoir
Elevation Gain: 1,740 feet; loss: 2,020 feet

Notes: This route to Uncle Bud's Hut, following the Glacier Creek Trail and the Colorado Trail, requires time, extreme attention to map and compass (a GPS is handy), advance skiing technique, and exceptional navigational skills. Allow plenty of time, as the trail is often not broken out and is difficult to follow. A safer alternate route (although 2.7 miles longer) is to follow the Glacier Creek Trail to Turquoise Lake Road (Road 104) from the Skinner Hut, continue to Road 107 and go left to Uncle Bud's Hut (see map and route 9.1). Although longer, this alternate route will probably even take less time, due to its following well-tracked roads. The description below is for the more complicated Colorado Trail route. A potential avalanche slope in Glacier Creek below the Skinner Hut should be monitored during high hazard periods, but is normally not a problem. Another potential hazard exists on the slopes on the skier's left before Galena Lake.

Route Description: From the Skinner Hut ski W for .3 miles down the ridge to the Hagerman Pass Road and look for the 10ᵗʰ Mountain marked trail on the right descending into the Glacier Creek drainage. The well-marked trail drops very steeply via switchbacks through the right side of the drainage. At 11,250 feet, the descent eases as you enter a large clearing. Stay right, heading E, and watch for the blue diamonds leading you down the creek drainage. After passing the steep rocky slope below the Skinner Hut, the trail again drops steeply down the gut of Glacier Creek, eventually coming out into a large clearing at 10,780 feet. Head ENE through the right side of the clearing, through about 150 feet of trees, and then into another large clearing. Head straight through the clearing to the far left end where the clearing curves left and the route exits the end of the clearing heading N.

From here the trail heads NE, dropping gently to a sharp left turn at 10,640 feet where you have to go left (NW) to avoid a precipitous drop. The trail traverses and switchbacks steeply down following blue diamonds and blazes marking the Colorado Trail to a junction with the Timberline Lake Trail at 10,110 feet (13S0375044E, 4349378N). Bear right, going downhill on the Colorado Trail for about 200 yards to a small open area (13S0375217E, 4349398N, 10,070 feet) with wooden fencing and trailhead signs. To continue to Uncle Bud's Hut go straight (ENE) on the marked 10th Mountain trail following the Colorado Trail. In about 100 feet the trail crosses a small bridge over a creek and then heads up into the trees on the blue diamond marked route.

The route traverses and then climbs N, soon entering the wilderness where the trail is only marked by blazes. Watch your map, compass and altimeter closely, as the trail is not very well marked in this section. At 10,600 feet the route turns E away from Mill Creek and follows the well-blazed trail that

Sunrise from the front of the Skinner Hut.

enters a large clearing at 11,090 feet (13S0376337E, 4350369N). Head left (N) up through the clearing and continue E to 11,430 feet (13S0376651E, 4350589N) to a ridge from where the marked trail begins its descent.

Follow the long switchbacking descent through trees, and then through an open area to traverse down to the right (E) side of an elongated lake at the base of a steep slope. Continue on a NE bearing to pass between the two Galena lakes and through the drainage above Bear Lake. (Do not drop down toward Bear Lake!). Continue the climb NE above the drainage on the blazed Colorado Trail, making sure to bear right at 11,265 feet (13S0378037E, 4351285N) on the blazed trail. At a signed trail intersection at 11,330 feet (13S0378314E, 4351301N) follow the Colorado Trail E for 150 yards to a large clearing (Bud's Gulch). Head E across the clearing to a blue diamond marked trail going up the slope on the other side ESE to Uncle Bud's Hut.

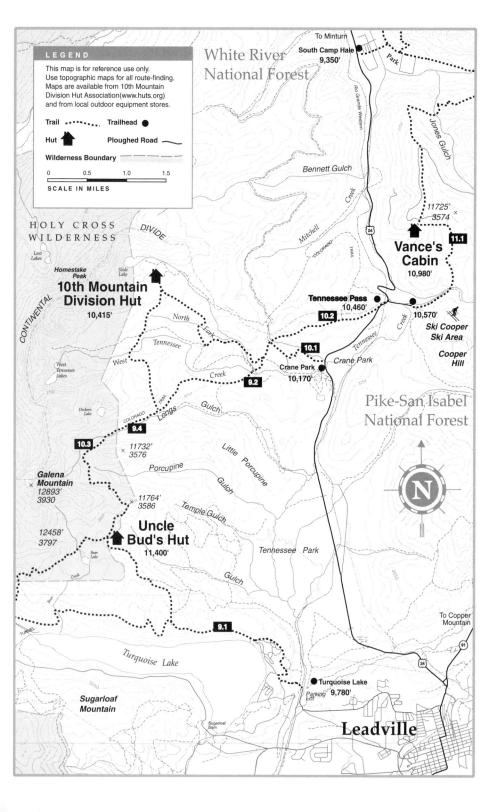

LEGEND

This map is for reference use only.
Use topographic maps for all route-finding.
Maps are available from 10th Mountain
Division Hut Association(www.huts.org)
and from local outdoor equipment stores.

Trail ·········   Trailhead ●

Hut 🏠   Ploughed Road ∿

Wilderness Boundary ∼∼∼∼∼

0   0.5   1.0   1.5

SCALE IN MILES

White River
National Forest

To Minturn

South Camp Hale
9,350'

Park

Rio Grande Western

Jones Gulch

Bennett Gulch

Mitchell

Creek

COLORADO TRAIL

11725'
3574

Vance's
Cabin
10,980'

11.1

HOLY CROSS
WILDERNESS

DIVIDE

Lost
Lakes

Homestake
Peak

Slide
Lake

10th Mountain
Division Hut
10,415'

North Fork

Tennessee

CONTINENTAL

West
Tennessee
Lakes

West

Creek

Tennessee Pass
10,460'

10.2

10.1

Crane Park
10,170'

Crane Park

9.2

10,570'

Ski Cooper
Ski Area

Cooper
Hill

Pike-San Isabel
National Forest

Deckers
Lake

COLORADO TRAIL

Longs

Gulch

9.4

10.3

11732'
3576

Galena
Mountain
12893'
3930

Porcupine

Little Porcupine

Gulch

11764'
3586

Temple Gulch

Gulch

12458'
3797

Bear Lake

Uncle
Bud's Hut
11,400'

Tennessee Park

Bear

Creek

Gulch

TUNNEL

9.1

To Copper
Mountain

91

24

Turquoise Lake

Turquoise Lake
Parking
Lot

Turquoise Lake
9,780'

Sugarloaf
Mountain

Sugarloaf
Dam

Leadville

N

Chapter 9 • Uncle Bud's Hut

Uncle Bud's Hut, located on the eastern flank of the Continental Divide at the foot of Galena Mountain, commands one of the best views of the surrounding mountains of any of the 10th Mountain huts. The hut is easily

Elevation: 11,400 feet
Coordinates: 13S0378812E, 4351163N
County: Lake
Access: Leadville

accessible by snow-covered roads from the Turquoise Lake Trailhead, but the longer route from the Crane Park Trailhead can be used, especially in conjunction with a loop route involving the 10th Mountain Division Hut. The hut-to-hut routes from Uncle Bud's to 10th Mountain Division Hut and to the Skinner Hut are scenic and challenging, true tests of the hutgoer's navigational skills. One of the primary attractions of Uncle Bud's is that the skiing around the hut offers something for everyone. Nearby St. Kevin's Gulch has wonderful easy and intermediate skiing, Peak 12,313 is a great peak for lots of good turns, and expert mountaineers can enjoy a day ascending and skiing Galena Mountain when snow conditions are right.

9.1 Turquoise Lake Trailhead to Uncle Bud's Hut

Difficulty: Intermediate
Distance: 5.8 miles
Time: 4-6 hours up; 3 hours down
Text Map: pp. 70, 78
10ᵗʰ Mtn Map: Continental Divide, Galena Mountain
USGS Map: Leadville North, Homestake Reservoir
Elevation Gain: 1,620 feet

Notes: The primary trailhead access to Uncle Bud's Hut follows all roads and involves very few navigational decisions.

Directions to Trailhead: From I-70 take Highway 24 or Highway 91 south to Leadville. At the north end of Leadville, turn W from Highway 24 onto Mountain View Drive (at the light by the Safeway store). Go 2.9 miles to a T-intersection (CR9) and turn right. Go .5 miles (staying right at the first fork) to a large parking area (13S0384448E, 4346969N, 9,780 feet) on the right side of the road.

Route Description: Walk across the highway onto the road (CR9) over the railroad tracks about 100 yards to the road closure and put on your skis. If you wax or have fish scales, skins won't be necessary for the first 3.5 miles. Follow the snow-covered road just over one-quarter mile to a T-intersection and turn right toward May Queen Campground. Continue following the main road, avoiding turns off to campgrounds and viewpoints, for another 3.2 miles on a gradual ascent. As the climb seems to peak, watch for Forest Service Road 107 going off to the right (13S0380509E, 4348798N, 10,445 feet). Put on your skins and begin your climb up Road 107. After several hundred yards, where FSR 103 goes right, stay straight on FSR 107. At another junction at 10,925 feet (13S0379873E, 4349850N) as a road goes down left, stay straight. The road flattens and drops slightly around 11,000 feet in an area of previous mining activity, with the remains of an old log cabin next to the road. Continue out of the mining area on the obvious road cut up a ridge NW to an intersection at 11,260 feet (13S0379100E, 4350926N) where the road goes left (W) and a trail continues straight. Go straight (NW) on the trail, steeply at first, then on a more level route NW through scattered pine trees to a clearing and the hut on the right.

Reverse Route: From the front of Uncle Bud's, head SE through the scattered pine trees, staying straight (SE) on Road 107 at 11,260 feet.

Follow the road SE for a mile into the flats at 11,000 feet where signs of mining activity still exist. Continue on FSR 107 on a steady descent another 1.1 miles to the intersection with Turquoise Lake Road, where you head left, staying on the main road for another 3.2 miles to the left turn for the last .3 miles to the trailhead.

9.2 Crane Park Trailhead to Uncle Bud's Hut

Difficulty: Intermediate/advanced
Distance: 8.3 miles
Time: 8-10 hours
Text Map: pp. 70, 78
10ᵗʰ Mtn Map: Continental Divide, Galena Mountain
USGS Map: Leadville North, Homestake Reservoir
Elevation Gain: 1,910 feet; loss: 680 feet

Notes: This route to Uncle Bud's is longer and more difficult to navigate than the route from Turquoise Lake, but it presents the experienced navigator a beautiful route over a trail that is often untracked beyond the initial section. Allow plenty of time and watch your map carefully; much of the route between Crane Park and the Lily Lake route can be confusing, and may change at some point in the future due to snowmobile and National Forest trail reroutes. Also, save some energy for the final 1,000-foot climb to the hut.

Dropping a second car off at the Turquoise Lake Trailhead can make this a good loop, allowing you to ski out on the easier route to Turquoise Lake. Be sure to stay on the 10ᵗʰ Mountain marked route on the steep slopes of the ridge to the north of Uncle Bud's Hut, and on the slope between Longs Gulch and Porcupine Gulch to avoid potential avalanche danger during high hazard periods.

Directions to Trailhead: From I-70: get off at Exit 171 (5 miles west of Vail) and take Highway 24 south for 25 miles (1.6 miles past Tennessee Pass) to a right turn onto a dirt road (County Road 19) where a sign on an old road grader indicates Webster Sand and Gravel Pit. A large parking area is immediately on the left by the trailhead (13S0385121E, 4356147N, 10,170 feet).

From Leadville: go N from the intersection of Highways 24 and 91 on Highway 24 for 7.5 miles to a left turn onto a dirt road where a sign on an old road grader indicates Webster Sand and Gravel Pit. Parking is on the left.

Route Description: From the trailhead, walk .3 miles W up the road to a road fork where the 10th Mountain marked trail begins and heads toward the creek. Cross over the creek and follow the trail along the right (N) side of the creek for a gradual ascent of just under a mile to the well-signed intersection (13S0383698E, 4356726N, 10,440 feet) with the trail coming from Tennessee Pass. Turn left (SE) to the right of a small gully towards the 10th Mountain Division Hut. After a short climb and a couple of curves you come to an intersection (13S0383672E, 4356559N, 10,510 feet) with Wurts Ditch Road. Go straight on the Colorado Trail (CT) and Continental Divide Trail (CDT) toward the 10th Mountain Division Hut. Beyond the intersection you come over a small knoll and drop on a sharp left through a clearing with young trees to a small gulch where you stay right along the gulch.

At a well-signed road crossing (13S0383326E, 4356264N, 10,390 feet) go straight to continue in a SW direction toward Uncle Bud's Hut. Bear SW through the edge of an open drainage and pick up the CT which soon curves to the W for a beautiful, gradual ascent for about 2 miles through the lodgepole pines. At an intersection (13S0380570E, 4355395N, 10,950 feet) with the trail heading NW toward the 10th Mountain Division Hut, continue straight (SW) on the CT on a gradual traversing, narrow downhill through the trees into Longs Gulch.

Go for about a mile along the north edge of Longs Gulch to the signed Holy Cross Wilderness boundary. One hundred yards beyond the sign the trail angles across the creek (13S0378801E, 4354201N) and up into the trees. (Do not continue in Longs Gulch!). The trail continues on a steady climb, getting steeper and steeper, to rise over a ridge (13S0378221E, 4353567N, 11,490 feet) into the open area at the head of Porcupine Gulch. Head S through the open area to where the trail enters the trees again (13S0378367E,

Entering the Holy Cross Wilderness in Longs Gulch.

4353223N, 11,300 feet). Traverse up through the trees to the base of a steep slope (13S0378711E, 4352752N, 11,440 feet) to begin a steep switchbacking ascent into the open area above timber line. Angle SE around the ridge through the open area to enter the trees again at 11,730 feet (13S0379011E, 4352177N). Follow the blazed trail as the trail curves around to the right (SW) and then S, gradually dropping through the trees. Upon entering the open area of Bud's Gulch, stay along the left edge, past the wilderness boundary, to a tree with a blue diamond (13S0378603E, 4351213N, 11,280 feet) from where you go left (ENE) up the slope for a 120-foot vertical climb to Uncle Bud's Hut at the top of a clearing. (Note: If you miss this turn, you will reach the signed Bear Lake Trailhead, about 200 feet past your turn).

Reverse Route: From the front of Uncle Bud's Hut go about 60 feet out into the clearing and then head WNW to drop down a slope into the open clearing (Bud's Gulch) to the west of the hut. Upon entering the clearing, turn right (N) and stay along the trees as you immediately cross the wilderness boundary and the trail will be marked by blazes. Continue N along the right side of the open area. At the end of the clearing the trail heads NNE on a climb through the trees. Watch carefully to follow the trail when it bears off to the right at about 11,600 feet, circling first NE and then back NW in the trees. As you break into the open above timber line, watch your map and compass carefully to follow a NW traverse around the ridge to a drop into a band of trees.

The trail continues to follow the Colorado Trail as it switchbacks steeply down through the trees. As the terrain flattens in Porcupine Gulch (13S0378440E, 4353144N, 11,300 feet), keep bearing left (NW). Continue NW, passing a couple of lakes in the open area, and begin to head NE for a traversing descent down through the trees into Longs Gulch. As you break into the open of Longs Gulch, you will immediately cross the creek (13S0378801E, 4354201N) and encounter the Holy Cross Wilderness boundary sign. The well-marked (blue diamonds) obvious trail continues on a traverse along Longs Gulch and starts climbing on a narrow track through the trees NE.

After the trail levels somewhat for about 200 yards, you reach a junction (13S0380570E, 4355395N, 10,950 feet) where the route to 10th Mountain Division Hut goes left, and the Colorado Trail goes right toward the Crane Park Trailhead. Continue from this junction on the CT heading NE and then E on a gradual descent through the lodgepole pines. Watch carefully for the CT going left at 10,715 feet (13S0381217E, 4355650N) where an old mine trail, generally used by snowmobiles, continues straight. Stay on the CT for a gradual downhill through the pines to an open area where you bear NE along a drainage. Continue heading NE as you come to numerous crossings and side routes in a potentially confusing section. Climb out of the drainage over a ridge, still heading NE. After dropping over the other side of the ridge you cross a bridge and come to the intersection of the Tennessee Pass and Crane Park trails (13S0383698E, 4356726N, 10,440 feet). Bear right down the drainage to head to Crane Park. The trail continues downhill along the left side of the drainage to a creek crossing just before exiting onto the road coming from the Crane Park Trailhead. Walk .3 miles E on the road to the trailhead.

9.3 Uncle Bud's Hut to Skinner Hut

Difficulty: Advanced
Distance: 7 miles/9.7 miles (alternate route)
Time: 8-10 hours
Text Map: p. 70
10th Mtn Map: Continental Divide
USGS Map: Homestake Reservoir
Elevation Gain: 2,020 feet: 1,740 feet

Notes: This route to the Skinner Hut, following the Colorado Trail and the Glacier Creek Trail, requires time, extreme attention to map and compass (a GPS is handy), advance skiing technique, and exceptional navigational skills. A safer alternate route (2.7 miles longer) is to follow Road 107 from Uncle Bud's Hut down to Road 104 and head W to the Glacier Creek Trail. Although longer, the alternate route will take no more time, due to its following well-tracked roads. Both alternatives end with a very steep climb up the Glacier Creek Trail, gaining 1,330 feet in elevation to the hut, so be prepared! A potential avalanche hazard exists on the slopes on the skier's right past Galena Lake. A potential avalanche slope in Glacier Creek below the Skinner Hut should be monitored during high hazard periods, but is normally not a problem. The description below is for the more difficult Colorado Trail route.

Route Description: From the front of Uncle Bud's Hut go about 60 feet out into the clearing and then head WNW to drop down a slope into the open clearing (Bud's Gulch) to the west of the hut. Head W across Bud's Gulch to where the Colorado Trail (marked by blazes) enters the woods on the other side of the open area. In about 150 yards, at a signed trail intersection (13S0378314E, 4351301N, 11,330 feet), follow the Colorado Trail south (angling off to left) to begin a steady descent. As you come to a bit of a gully (13S0378037E, 4351285N, 11,265 feet) make sure to drop down left on the Colorado Trail, and not continue up to the right (both directions have blazes). When you drop into the open area above Bear Lake, avoid the temptation to follow the drainage SSE. Instead, stay on a SW bearing to cross the creek and head into the trees where you go W between the two Galena lakes and skirt the left side of an elongated lake up against the base of Galena Mountain.

Continue on a steady climb through the open area beyond the lake and into the trees on a steadily climbing, switchbacking, blazed trail. After reaching the high point on the ridge at 11,430 feet (13S0376651E, 4350589N), drop down into a clearing. It's a chance to take some turns, but stay right and avoid the temptation to ski too far down the clearing. At 11,090 feet (13S0376337E, 4350369N) go into the trees on the right and look for a blazed trail (this turn is not well marked). Follow the blazed trail as it steadily switchbacks down in the trees. At 10,600 feet, just before reaching Mill Creek, the trail turns S. Watch you map and compass closely, as the trail is poorly marked from here, and may be difficult to follow. As the trail leaves the wilderness, it is again marked by blue diamonds as it traverses W down the last section to a creek crossing on a small wooden bridge and a small open area with wooden fencing and trailhead signs (13S0375217E, 4349398N, 10,070 feet).

From this point, follow the Colorado Trail (W) uphill about 200 yards to the Timberline Lake Trailhead. Take a left (W) on the blue diamond marked trail at the "Closed to all Motor Vehicles" sign (do not follow the Timberline Lake Trail). Continue on a steady steep switchbacking and traversing ascent to a right turn in a small clearing at 10,640 feet. Continue SW. At the large clearing at 10,760 feet stay on a WSW bearing into an outcropping of trees and then into a second clearing. Angle to the left through the clearing onto the marked trail in the trees. From here you ascend up a small gully quite steeply, winding up to an open area at 11,160 feet below the rock faces beneath the hut. A gradual ascent through a couple of small open areas quickly leads to the final steep switchbacking ascent to the Hagerman Pass Road at the head of the Glacier Creek drainage. Go E up the ridge on the left for the last .3 miles to the Skinner Hut.

9.4 Uncle Bud's Hut to 10ᵗʰ Mountain Division Hut

Difficulty: Intermediate/advanced
Distance: 7.3 miles
Time: 7-9 hours
Text Map: pp. 70, 78
10ᵗʰ Mtn Map: Galena Mountain
USGS Map: Homestake Reservoir
Elevation Gain: 1,505 feet; loss: 1,490 feet

Notes: This very scenic, rewarding, yet quite demanding hut-to-hut route follows the Colorado Trail most of the way to the 10ᵗʰ Mountain Division Hut. The route, which parallels the Continental Divide, dips in and out of a number of drainages and requires good navigational skills and a lot of attention to compass, altimeter and map. The marked route around Peak 12,313 should be followed carefully to avoid getting onto potential avalanche slopes. Also, be sure to stay on the 10ᵗʰ Mountain marked route on the slope between Longs Gulch and Porcupine Gulch to avoid potential avalanche danger during high hazard periods. The trail is often unbroken, especially after storms, so allow plenty of extra time under these conditions.

Route Description: From the front of Uncle Bud's Hut go about 60 feet out into the clearing and then head WNW to drop down a slope into the open clearing (Bud's Gulch) to the west of the hut. Upon entering the

A view from the trail between Uncle Bud's and 10ᵗʰ Mountain Division huts.

clearing, turn right (N) and stay along the trees as you immediately cross the wilderness boundary. The trail will now be marked by blazes in the wilderness area. Continue N along the right side of the open area to the trail heading NNE on a climb through the trees from the end of the clearing. Watch carefully to follow the trail when it bears off to the right at about 11,600 feet, circling first NE and then back NW in the trees. As you break into the open above timber line, watch your map and compass carefully to follow a NW traverse around the ridge to a drop into a band of trees. The trail follows the Colorado Trail switchbacking very steeply down through the trees (this section requires extra caution and possibly skins for less experienced skiers).

As the terrain flattens in Porcupine Gulch (13S0378440E, 4353144N, 11,300 feet), keep bearing left (NW). Continue NW, passing a couple of lakes in the open area, and begin to head NE for a traversing descent down through the trees into Longs Gulch. As you break into the open of Longs Gulch, you will immediately cross the creek (13S0378801E, 4354201N) and encounter the Holy Cross Wilderness boundary sign. The well-marked (blue diamonds) obvious trail continues on a traverse along Longs Gulch for a mile and then starts climbing on a narrow track through the trees NE. After the trail levels somewhat for about 200 yards, you reach a junction (13S0380570E, 4355395N, 10,950 feet) where the route to 10th Mountain Division Hut goes left, and the Colorado Trail goes right toward the Crane Park Trailhead.

Go left and continue NNW on an easy ascent to a flat, open area. Stay on a NW heading to climb the ridge on the other side of the clearing via some short switchbacks. The marked trail descends gradually off the ridge as it turns W through the trees and enters an open area. Stay along the right side of the area, curving N and up to a gap at the top of a hillock. Drop N down the other side of the hillock to the large open area (13S0379618E, 4356710N, 11,080 feet) of West Tennessee Creek. Check your compass and take a NE bearing to cross the drainage and to pick up the trail going into the woods on the other side.

The trail continues through the trees NNE, climbing a ridge to 11,160 feet and then dropping into the head of North Fork West Tennessee Creek. Follow the trail N up through a clearing on the other side of the creek and head NNE through the trees into a large clearing. Head NE through the clearing to the hut boundary sign and then 200 feet N to the 10th Mountain Division Hut.

Chapter 10 • 10th Mountain Division Hut

The popular 10th Mountain Division Hut sits just below the Continental Divide and Homestake Peak in one of the most spectacular settings for any hut in the 10th Mountain Hut System. An abundance of ski terrain for all levels exists around the hut, ranging

Elevation: 11,415 feet
Coordinates: 13S0380532E, 4358641N
County: Lake
Access: Highway 24, Leadville/Minturn

from easier bowls and slopes near the hut, to expert terrain on the Continental Divide, especially on the cone-shaped Homestake Peak. Tours to the nearby Slide Lake area are popular, as is the spectacular climb up Homestake Peak. Getting to this hut can be a navigational headache due to the many different types of trails that exist along the route from the two trailheads. Snowmobile trails are plentiful (usually marked with orange diamonds), some of the Forest Service trails in the area are marked with blue diamonds similar to the 10th Mountain trails, and the maps sometimes reflect old and non-existent trails. Needless to say, careful attention to the maps and compass readings is a must, and be aware that trails may be occasionally rerouted. A GPS would certainly be a great aid along these routes.

10.1 Crane Park Trailhead to 10th Mountain Division Hut

Difficulty: Intermediate
Distance: 4.4 miles
Time: 4-5 hours up; 3 hours down
Text Map: pp. 70, 78
10th Mtn Map: Galena Mountain
USGS Map: Homestake Reservoir, Leadville North
Elevation Gain: 1,445 feet; loss: 200 feet

Notes: The route from the Crane Park Trailhead to the 10th Mountain Division Hut is the shortest access, but not the most scenic. It involves walking .3 miles along the road to get to the ski trail, and the first part of the route might have a few bare spots during periods of low snow. For a slightly longer, but much more interesting route, use the route from Tennessee Pass (10.2). Allow plenty of time and watch your map carefully; much of the route, especially in the Lily Lake area, can be confusing, and may change at some point due to snowmobile and National Forest trail reroutes. Cars should park right off Highway 24 in the Crane Park Trailhead parking area, and not attempt to drive up the road to find parking.

Directions to Trailhead: From I-70 get off at Exit 171 (5 miles west of Vail) and take Highway 24 south for 25 miles (1.6 miles past Tennessee Pass) to a right turn onto a dirt road (County Road 19) where a sign on an old road grader indicates Webster Sand and Gravel Pit. A large parking area is on the left by the trailhead (13S0385121E, 4356147N, 10,170 feet).

From Leadville go north from the intersection of Hwy 24 and 91 on Highway 24 for 7.5 miles to a left turn onto a dirt road where a sign on an old road grader indicates Webster Sand and Gravel Pit. Parking is on the left.

Route Description: From the trailhead, walk .3 miles W up the road to a road fork where the 10th Mountain marked trail begins and heads toward the creek. Cross over the creek and follow the trail along the right (N) side of the creek for a gradual ascent of just under a mile to the well-signed intersection (13S0383698E, 4356726N, 10,440 feet) with the trail coming from Tennessee Pass. Turn left (SE) towards the 10th Mountain Division Hut. After a short climb and a couple of curves you come to an intersection (13S0383672E, 4356559N, 10,510 feet) with Wurts Ditch Road. Go straight on the Colorado Trail (CT) and Continental Divide Trail (CDT). Beyond the intersection the route goes over a small knoll and drops down sharply to the left through a clearing with young trees and follows the right side of a small gulch.

At a well-signed road crossing at 10,390 feet (13S0383326E, 4356264N) go right on the marked trail on Road 131. Stay straight on Road 131 as it intersects (13S0382912E, 4356261N, 10,425 feet) with the Lily Lake Loop Trail. At a large clearing head through the left edge NNW, and at the far edge put on your skins for the uphill climb (13S0382077E, 4357035N, 10,625 feet). Go up a steep section through the woods; as the trail flattens out somewhat, continue through some open areas, gradually heading NW toward the Continental Divide ahead. Continue NW on the right edge of a large open clearing. As the edge of the clearing turns north, take the last gradual ascent N to the hut.

Reverse Route: From the 10th Mountain Division Hut, go south along the left edge of the large clearing and bear SE along the clearing's edge as it curves left. Continue SE through open areas on a gradual descent to about 10,770 feet where you turn SW and descend a steep section to a large clearing at 10,625 feet. Head SSE through the clearing to a left on the other side onto Road 131 heading E. Follow this road as it turns to the SE, not making the turn onto the Lily Lake Loop Trail. Watch your compass carefully as this section can have confusing turns and trails.

At 10,390 feet go left onto the trail heading ENE up over a ridge and down into a gulch where the Tennessee Pass and Crane Park trails intersect at 10,440 feet (13S0383698E, 4356726N) just over a small bridge. Bear right down the drainage to head to Crane Park. The trail continues downhill along the left side of the drainage to a creek crossing just before exiting onto the road coming from the Crane Park Trailhead. Walk .3 miles E on the road to the trailhead.

10.2 Tennessee Pass Trailhead to 10th Mountain Division Hut

Difficulty: Intermediate
Distance: 5.7 miles
Time: 5-6 hours up; 3-4 hours down
Text Map: pp. 70, 78
10th Mtn Map: Galena Mountain
USGS Map: Homestake Reservoir, Leadville North
Elevation Gain: 1,245 feet; loss: 290 feet

Notes: Although this route, beginning along the Colorado Trail, is not the shortest route to the 10th Mountain Division Hut, it is the most scenic and most convenient; therefore it is the recommended route to the hut. The bathrooms at the trailhead are an added incentive to use this route instead of Crane Park. Allow plenty of time and watch your map carefully; much of the route, especially in the Lily Lake area, can be confusing, and may change at some point due to snowmobile and National Forest trail reroutes. This route is also used as part of the ski-through to and from Vance's Cabin.

Directions to Trailhead: From I-70 get off at Exit 171 (5 miles west of Vail) and take Highway 24 south for 23.3 miles to the well-signed Tennessee Pass and the entrance to Ski Cooper.

From the intersection of highways 24 and 91 in Leadville go 9 miles north on Highway 24 to Tennessee Pass.

Turn into the large parking area on the west side of the highway and park. The parking area is equipped with bathrooms. The trailhead is located on the west side of the parking area (13S0387030E, 4357844N, 10,460 feet).

Route Description: The marked trail meanders through the trees, following the Colorado Trail (CT) and Continental Divide Trail (CDT). No skins are necessary. At the intersection with the Treeline Trail stay straight on the CT. In a little over one mile the trail comes to a well-marked intersection (13S0383698E, 4356726N, 10,440 feet) with the Crane Park Trail at a bridge over a creek. Cross over the bridge and go straight (a sharp left takes you back to Crane Park) and bear left (SE) to the right of a small gully towards the 10th Mountain Division Hut. After a short climb and a couple of curves you come to an intersection (13S0383672E, 4356559N, 10,510 feet) with Wurts Ditch Road. Go straight on the Colorado Trail (CT) and Continental Divide Trail (CDT).

Beyond the intersection the route goes over a small knoll and drops down sharply to the left through a clearing with young trees and follows the right side of a small gulch. At a well-signed road crossing at 10,390 feet (13S0383326E, 4356264N) go right on the marked trail on Road 131. Stay straight on Road 131 as it intersects (13S0382912E, 4356261N, 10,425 feet) with the Lily Lake Loop Trail.

At a large clearing head through the left edge NNW, and at the far edge put on your skins for the uphill climb (13S0382077E, 4357035N, 10,625 feet). Go up a steep section through the woods; as the trail flattens out somewhat, continue through some open areas, gradually heading NW toward the Continental Divide ahead. Continue NW on the right edge of a large open clearing. As the edge of the clearing turns north, take the last gradual ascent N to the hut.

Reverse Route: From the 10th Mountain Division Hut, go south along the left edge of the large clearing and bear SE along the clearing's edge as it curves left. Continue SE through open areas on a gradual descent to about 10,770 feet where you turn SW and descend a steep section to a large clearing at 10,625 feet. Head SSE through the clearing to a left on the other side onto Road 131 heading E. Follow this road as it turns to the SE, not making the turn onto the Lily Lake Loop Trail. Watch your compass carefully as this section can have confusing turns and trails.

At 10,390 feet go left onto the trail heading ENE up over a ridge and down into a gulch where the Tennessee Pass and Crane Park trails

intersect at 10,440 feet (13S0383698E, 4356726N) just over a small bridge. Stay straight toward Tennessee Pass. Continue ENE on a pleasant traverse through the trees on the CT/CDT trails for the last 2.4 miles to Tennessee Pass.

Inside the 10th Mountain Division Hut.

10.3 10ᵗʰ Mountain Division Hut to Uncle Bud's Hut

Difficulty: Intermediate/advanced
Distance: 7.3 miles
Time: 7-9 hours
Text Map: pp. 70, 78
10ᵗʰ Mtn Map: Galena Mountain
USGS Map: Homestake Reservoir
Elevation Gain: 1,490 feet; loss: 1,505 feet

Notes: This very scenic, rewarding, yet quite demanding hut-to-hut route follows the Colorado Trail much of the way to Uncle Bud's Hut. The route dips in and out of a number of drainages and requires good navigational skills and a lot of attention to compass, altimeter and map. Be sure to stay on the 10ᵗʰ Mountain marked route on the slope between Longs Gulch and Porcupine Gulch to avoid potential avalanche danger during high hazard periods. Also, the marked route around Peak 12,313 should be followed carefully to avoid getting onto potential avalanche slopes. The trail is often unbroken, especially after storms, so allow plenty of extra time under these conditions.

Route Description: Go south from the 10ᵗʰ Mountain Division Hut about 200 feet to the hut boundary sign and turn due SW across the open area to enter the trees where the trail is marked by a blue diamond. After climbing a little the trail drops S through a clearing into North Fork West Tennessee Creek, down through the woods and up the other side. From a high point of 11,160 feet you then drop down S into the broad, wide, open expanse of West Tennessee Creek. Use your compass to take a SW bearing to cross the creek and to continue SW to a slight open hillside (13S0379618E, 4356710N, 11,080 feet), where you curve up left to the gap at the top of the hillock. Here you break through the trees into a large clearing and curve left to head E along the left side of the open area before entering the woods again. As the trail bears SE you summit a ridge and take a steep downhill into a flat clearing. Continue SSE on an easy descent to the junction with the CT at 10,950 feet (13S0380570E, 4355395N) where you stay straight toward Uncle Bud's Hut.

Continue SW on a gradual traversing, narrow downhill through the trees into Longs Gulch. Go for about a mile along the north edge of Longs Gulch to the signed Holy Cross Wilderness boundary. One hundred yards beyond the sign the trail angles across the creek (13S0378801E,

4354201N) and up into the trees. (Do not continue in Longs Gulch!). The trail continues on a steady climb, getting steeper and steeper, to rise over a ridge (13S0378221E, 4353567N, 11,490 feet) into the open area at the head of Porcupine Gulch. Head S through the clearing to where the trail enters the trees again (13S0378367E, 4353223N, 11,300 feet). Traverse up through the trees to the base of a steep slope (13S0378711E, 4352752N, 11,440 feet) to begin a steep switchbacking ascent into the open area above timber line. Angle SE around the ridge to enter the trees again at 11,730 feet (13S0379011E, 4352177N). Follow the blazed trail as the trail curves around to the right (SW) and then S, gradually dropping through the trees. Upon entering the open area of Bud's Gulch, stay along the left edge, past the wilderness boundary, to a tree with a blue diamond (13S0378603E, 4351213N, 11,280 feet) from where you go left (ENE) up the slope for a 120-foot vertical climb to Uncle Bud's Hut. (Note: If you skied past this turn, you will reach the signed Bear Lake Trailhead, 200 feet past your turn).

10.4 10ᵗʰ Mountain Division Hut to Vance's Cabin

Difficulty: Intermediate
Distance: 8.8 miles
Time: 8-9 hours
Text Map: p. 78
10ᵗʰ Mtn Map: Galena Mountain, Chicago Ridge
USGS Map: Homestake Reservoir, Leadville North, Pando
Elevation Gain: 1,010 feet; loss: 1,445 feet

Notes: This route, normally part of a long ski-through, involves crossing Highway 24 at Tennessee Pass, and therefore arrangements can be made for a food drop if needed. Many people, however, break their trip at Highway 24.

Route Description: From the 10ᵗʰ Mountain Division Hut, go south along the left edge of the large clearing and bear SE along the clearing's edge as it curves left. Continue SE through open areas on a gradual descent to about 10,770 feet where you turn SW and descend a steep section to a large clearing at 10,625 feet. Head SSE through the clearing to a left on the other side onto Road 131 heading E. Follow this road as it turns to the SE, not making the turn onto the Lily Lake Loop Trail. Watch your compass carefully as this section can have confusing turns and trails. At 10,390 feet go left onto the trail heading ENE up over a ridge and down into a gulch where the Tennessee Pass and Crane

Park trails intersect at 10,440 feet (13S0383698E, 4356726N) just over a small bridge. Stay straight toward Tennessee Pass. Continue ENE on a pleasant traverse through the trees on the CT/CDT trails for the last 2.4 miles to Tennessee Pass. From Tennessee Pass, take off your skis and cross Highway 24 to the entrance to the Ski Cooper ski area. Walk/ski .5 miles up the entrance road to the Vance's Cabin trailhead (13S0387804E, 4357643N, 10,570 feet) on the left side of the Ski Cooper parking lot.

From the Vance's Cabin trailhead follow the road cut used as part of the Nordic trail system as it traverses ENE above Piney Gulch. In just over ½ mile, as the road rises to the right, stay left to cross the creek and you will slowly ascend N through an open area to the left of Piney Gulch. In about ¼ mile the route heads up steeply to the left (NW) through an open area on the left side of a shallow secondary gulch. At the far end of the open area, after a steep climb, the route enters the woods first in a WNW direction, then soon heads north for a gradual climb in the trees for almost a mile. At 11,400 feet you come to a small open area with some scattered trees. Traverse into the open area, go left (W) and ski down, watching for tree stumps, dropping about 200 feet in elevation to the hut on the left.

Homestake Peak on the Continental Divide and the 10ᵗʰ Mountain Division Hut.

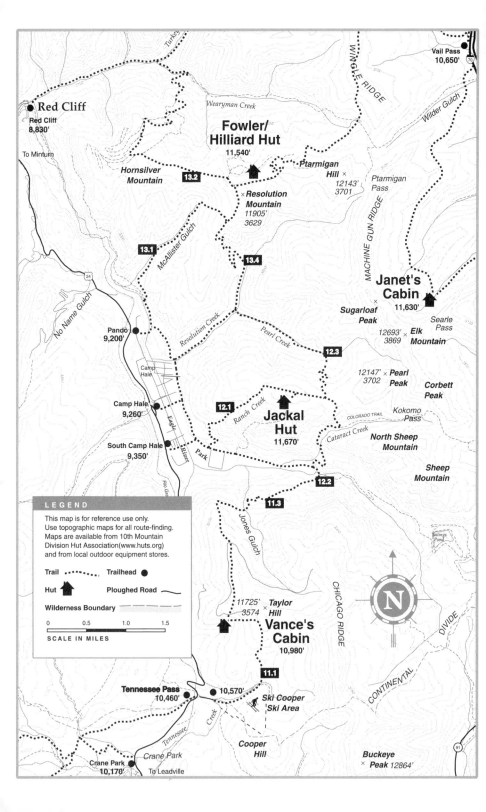

Chapter 11 • Vance's Cabin

Vance's Cabin, easily accessible from Ski Cooper at Tennessee Pass, is a good choice for novice hutgoers. Vance's Cabin is a quaint, privately owned hut, small and somewhat weathered, but certainly located in an idyllic setting looking out from its forested ridge onto the

Elevation: 10,980 feet
Coordinates: 13S0388050E, 4360105N
County: Summit
Access: From Ski Cooper at Tennessee Pass north of Leadville

surrounding mountains. The hut has three levels, with a sauna on the lowest level, and has gas lights and a gas stove. Space in the hut is definitely limited and tight.

The closest place to make some easy turns is the area right above the hut, with Taylor Hill to the east being a good destination for a short tour and mellow turns. Ski-throughs to either the 10th Mountain Division Hut or the Jackal Hut are possible for the more experienced hutgoers, with the trip to Jackal being one of the more demanding ski-through trips in the system.

11.1 Tennessee Pass Trailhead to Vance's Cabin

Difficulty: Beginner/intermediate
Distance: 2.6 miles
Time: 3 hours up, 2 hours down
Text Map: pp. 78, 96
10th Mtn Map: Chicago Ridge
USGS Map: Leadville North, Pando
Elevation Gain: 610 feet; loss 200 feet

Notes: This short route to the hut is ideal for a beginning hut route. The only other access is the long route from Camp Hale or from the Jackal Hut. Trail-finding is relatively easy, but care should still be taken, especially closer to the hut and during bad weather.

Directions to Trailhead: From I-70 get off at Exit 171 (5 miles west of Vail) and take Highway 24 south for 23.3 miles to the well-signed Tennessee Pass and the entrance to Ski Cooper.

From the intersection of highways 24 and 91 in Leadville, go 9 miles north on Highway 24 to the well-signed Tennessee Pass and the entrance to Ski Cooper.

Turn in on the road to Ski Cooper and go .5 miles to the large parking lot and the 10th Mountain parking on the left (13S0387804E, 4357643N, 10,570 feet) for Vance's Cabin across from the cross-country touring center. Park only in the 10th Mountain designated parking area along the bank; do not park anywhere else in the Ski Cooper parking area.

Route Description: From trailhead parking follow the road cut used as part of the Nordic trail system as it traverses ENE above Piney Gulch. In just over ½ mile, as the road rises to the right, stay left to cross the creek and you will slowly ascend N through an open area to the left of Piney Gulch. In about ¼ mile the route heads up steeply to the left (NW) through an open area on the left side of a shallow secondary gulch.

At the far end of the open area, after a steep climb, the route enters the woods first in a WNW direction, then soon heads north for a gradual climb in the trees for almost a mile. At 11,400 feet you come to a small open area with some scattered trees. Traverse into the open area, go left (W) and ski down along the left edge of the open area, watching for tree stumps, dropping about 200 feet in elevation to the hut.

Reverse Route: Use your skins, head up (ENE) through the open clearing above the cabin, staying along the right side. At the top of the clearing watch carefully for the trail going off to the right (ESE) into the woods. Once on this trail you can take off your skins and follow the clear, well-marked cut through the trees as it slowly descends for a little over a mile, breaking out into an open area where you ski down into Piney Gulch. Follow the trail on the right of the gulch for about ¼ mile to the creek crossing and then go right (SW) on the wide Nordic trail above the gulch for the last ½ mile to the trailhead in the Ski Cooper parking area.

11.2 Vance's Cabin to 10th Mountain Division Hut

Difficulty: Intermediate
Distance: 8.8 miles
Time: 8-9 hours
Text Map: p. 78
10th Mtn Map: Galena Mountain, Chicago Ridge
USGS Map: Homestake Reservoir, Leadville North, Pando
Elevation Gain: 1,445 feet; loss: 1,010 feet

Notes: This route, normally part of a long ski-through, involves crossing Highway 24 at Tennessee Pass, and therefore arrangements can be made for a food drop if needed. Many people, however, break their trip at Highway 24.

Route Description: Use your skins, head up (ENE) through the open clearing above the cabin, staying along the right side. At the top of the clearing watch carefully for the trail going off to the right (ESE) into the woods. Once on this trail you can take off your skins and follow the clear, well-marked cut through the trees as it slowly descends for a little over a mile, breaking out into an open area where you ski down into Piney Gulch. Follow the trail on the right of the gulch for about ¼ mile to the creek crossing and then go right (SW) on the wide Nordic trail above the gulch for the last ½ mile to the trailhead in the Ski Cooper parking area.

Go right and walk/ski .5 miles out the Ski Cooper entrance road to Highway 24. Cross the highway to the Tennessee Pass Trailhead (13S0387030E, 4357844N, 10,460 feet) for the 10th Mountain Division Hut in the parking lot on the other side of the highway. Follow the marked trail out of the parking lot as it meanders through the trees, following the Colorado Trail (CT) and Continental Divide Trail (CDT). No skins are necessary. At the intersection with the Treeline Trail stay straight on the CT. In a little over one mile the trail comes to a well-marked intersection (13S0383698E, 4356726N, 10,440 feet) with the Crane Park Trail at a bridge over a creek. Cross over the bridge and go straight (a sharp left takes you back to Crane Park) and bear left (SE) to the right of a small gully towards the 10ᵗʰ Mountain Division Hut.

After a short climb and a couple of curves you come to an intersection (13S0383672E, 4356559N, 10,510 feet) with Wurts Ditch Road. Go straight on the Colorado Trail (CT) and Continental Divide Trail (CDT). Beyond the intersection the route goes over a small knoll and drops down sharply to the left through a clearing with young trees and follows the right side of a small gulch.

At a well-signed road crossing at 10,390 feet (13S0383326E, 4356264N) go right on the marked trail on Road 131. Stay straight on the Road 131 as it intersects (13S0382912E, 4356261N, 10,425 feet) with the Lily Lake Loop Trail. At a large clearing head through the left edge NNW, and at the far edge put on your skins for the uphill climb (13S0382077E, 4357035N, 10,625 feet). Go up a steep section through the woods; as the trail flattens out somewhat continue through some open areas, gradually heading NW toward the Continental Divide ahead. Continue NW on the right edge of a large open clearing. As the edge of the clearing turns north, take the last gradual ascent N to the hut.

11.3 Vance's Cabin to Jackal Hut

Difficulty: Intermediate/advanced
Distance: 8.5 miles
Time: 8-10 hours
Text Map: p. 96
10ᵗʰ Mtn Map: Chicago Ridge
USGS Map: Pando
Elevation Gain: 2,250 feet; loss: 1,560 feet

Notes: Getting from Vance's Cabin to the Jackal Hut via Cataract Creek is one of the more difficult routes in the entire hut system, due largely to the 2,000-foot climb in the last 3.4 miles to the hut. Good navigational skills are definitely necessary on this last section of the route. If you have a choice, plan your trip to go from Jackal to Vance's, so that the most difficult section can be gotten out of the way sooner, and the elevation gain at the end is less. During periods of high avalanche hazard the steep slope to the west of the trail above the Cataract Creek crossing can present a danger. Watch for a marked route to the east to avoid this hazard.

Route Description: Head from the hut buildings E on a slightly rising traverse to the trail entering the trees on the west side of the clearing and follow it heading N into the trees, making sure not to drop down on the road cuts going off to the left. In .7 miles continue right on a level, traversing road cut as the trail ends. In another .6 miles, at the road/trail intersection (13S0388057E, 4362102N), bear left onto the trail and follow it N as it drops along the crest of the ridge for .9 miles to 10,670 feet and a sharp right turn (13S0387657E, 4363122N). Continue on a slightly dropping traverse ESE to a large open area. Follow the left edge of the open area to Jones Gulch. Drop down steeply through the gulch to a flat area in the trees and continue E on the trail to some descending switchbacks at 10,200 feet.

Continue the descent on the well-marked trail another 1½ miles through the trees to the open area of East Fork drainage, crossing it NW to the snowmobile-packed road (13S0390762E, 4363988N, 9,585 feet). Go left on the road one-quarter mile to a trail on the right by a small wooden fence (13S0393488E, 4364213N). Go right (NE) on the trail through an open area to pick up the Colorado Trail at the other end of the clearing. Go right on the Colorado Trail on a narrow climbing traverse as it soon turns N and crosses Cataract Creek at 10,140 feet (13S0390709E, 4364831N). A couple of quick switchbacks takes you up above Cataract Creek to an ascending traverse first N, then W, above the creek. On entering a clearing at 10,740 feet (13S0391615E, 4365416N), turn N for a 660-foot vertical climb due N through the open areas on the left side of a gulch.

At 11,400 feet (13S0391527E, 4366060N) go left (W), to head up through a sloped open area. Continue W along the ridge to a saddle at 11,420 feet (13S030959E, 4366119N), where the trail to Pearl Creek heads off to the right (N). Do not take this trail, but stay straight (W) to make a gradual ascent along a ridge for .6 miles to the 10th Mountain summer parking area, from where you drop slightly for a couple of hundred feet to the Jackal Hut at the edge of some trees just below the summit.

Chapter 12 • Jackal Hut

The Jackal Hut, named after Jack (Schuss) and Al (Zesiger), sits on the south face of a beautiful summit, commanding views of the Tennessee Pass area, 14,000-foot peaks of the Sawatch Range, and the Elk Ridge to the east. The skiing near the hut is

Elevation: 11,670 feet
Coordinates: 13S0390054E, 4366191N
County: Eagle
Access: Camp Hale, Highway 24

good, with open slopes and glades right around the hut. For ski mountaineers nearby Pearl Peak and the Elk Ridge offer opportunities to explore over 12,000 feet.

Both the Jackal Hut and the Fowler/Hilliard Hut are constructed similarly, and these two huts form a good circuit from Camp Hale for stays in the spectacular high country above Camp Hale. The Jackal Hut is easily accessed from the South Camp Hale Trailhead via Ranch Creek. The hut-to-hut trips from Jackal to either Fowler/Hilliard to the north, or Vance's to the south, are scenic, but long and somewhat difficult.

12.1 South Camp Hale Trailhead to Jackal Hut

Difficulty: Intermediate
Distance: 4 miles
Time: 4-5 hours up; 2-3 hours down
Text Map: p. 96
10ᵗʰ Mtn Map: Chicago Ridge
USGS Map: Pando
Elevation Gain: 2,320 feet

Notes: This efficient access that climbs steeply to the Jackal Hut from Camp Hale follows the Ranch Creek drainage along an obvious road cut, making navigation relatively easy, although it's still important to watch the map closely, especially at the beginning and the end of the route. As always, be aware of snowmobiles at the beginning of the route in Camp Hale.

Directions to Trailhead: From I-70 turn off at the Minturn exit (Exit 171) 5 miles west of Vail and go south for 18 miles to a parking area (13S0386297E, 4364001N, 9,350 feet) right next to the road on the left at the south end of the Camp Hale flats.

From the intersection of highways 24 and 91 just north of Leadville, drive north on Highway 24 for 14.4 miles to the parking area for the South Camp Hale Trailhead parking area on the right side of the road. Note that this trailhead is a part of the Vail Pass Recreation Area and a use fee is required. This fee is included in your fee for the hut, so have a copy of your hut waiver on you to show that you have paid.

Route Description: From the back of the parking area head east and cross the Eagle River on a snow-covered wooden foot bridge. Continue straight (ENE) to the wide road at the base of the mountain on the east side of Camp Hale and turn right. Follow the road for one-quarter mile to a well-signed intersection (13S0387428E, 4364829N, 9,330 feet) with Ranch Creek Road 755 which heads up to the left (NE) through an open area into the Ranch Creek drainage. Put on your skins and head up the Ranch Creek Road as it switchbacks through the open area towards a drainage. If the road is too snow-covered to follow easily, then head toward the drainage, staying left of the bushes above, watching for the road traversing along the hillside above and to the left. Continue into some trees, another open area (where you angle up ENE), go through a few aspen trees at 10,030 feet, exit the next open area at 10,220 feet

103

(13S0387924E, 4365671N), and then follow the Ranch Creek drainage on a fairly steep winding ascent to a ridge at 11,240 feet. Follow the ridge E to 11,720 feet (its summit) from where you drop down SW the last 100 yards to the hut at the top of the open area below a few trees on the south side of the ridge.

Reverse Route: From the back of the hut traverse up N to the top of the ridge above the hut and head W along the ridge. After a gentle descent along the open area on the ridge, the route drops into the trees and continues on a somewhat steep, winding, well-marked jeep road, dropping along Ranch Creek. When the road breaks into the open, Camp Hale is visible ahead. Continue following the road (Ranch Creek Road 755) as it switchbacks down through some more trees and open area to Camp Hale. At the intersection (13S0387428E, 4364829N, 9,330 feet) with the wide road that goes along the base of the mountain in Camp Hale, turn right for about one-quarter mile to where the road passes through a wooden fence/gate and a road track (13S0387068E, 4365080N, 9,300 feet) goes off to the left (WNW) toward the Eagle River and the highway. Go left, and cross the Eagle River on a snow-covered wooden foot bridge to reach the South Camp Hale Trailhead.

12.2 Jackal Hut to Vance's Cabin

Difficulty: Intermediate/advanced
Distance: 8.5 miles
Time: 8-9 hours
Text Map: p. 96
10ᵗʰ Mtn Map: Chicago Ridge
USGS Map: Pando
Elevation Gain: 1,560 feet; loss: 2,250 feet

Notes: This route, which drops into the Cataract Creek drainage, is the most scenic and efficient way between the Jackal Hut and Vance's Cabin. It follows trail virtually the entire way, and good navigational skills are a must, as junctions in open areas can easily be missed. Advanced skiers have a chance to make turns on the drop towards Cataract Creek, although snow conditions on the south-facing slope can be difficult. The route is long and arduous, with a good climb in the second half, so start early. In periods of high avalanche hazard the steep slope west of the trail above the Cataract Creek crossing can present a danger. Watch for a marked route to the east to avoid this hazard.

Route Description: From the Jackal Hut, traverse up the ridge E to the 10ᵗʰ Mountain summer parking area and a marked route. Head down the ridge E about three-quarters mile to a saddle at 11,420 feet (13S0390959E, 4366119N, shortly after entering the trees). Continue straight (E) along the ridge in the trees as the trail rises slightly and then drops somewhat. Stay E along the right side of the ridge into a large sloped open area to a point where a blue diamond on a tree marks a sharp right turn downhill (13S0391527E, 4366060N, 11,400 feet).

Continue due S in the open area along the right side of the drainage. If snow conditions are good this is a chance to get in some good turns, but take care not to go too far right. Stay as close to the gulch as possible, and soon you will be right along the creek bed. Down toward the bottom of the clearings at 10,740 feet watch for a marked trail going off to the right (WSW) into the trees (13S0391615E, 4365416N). Continue on this well-marked Colorado Trail as it traverses above Cataract Creek, first in the trees, and then across some open slopes.

The Jackal Hut front porch.

At 10,240 feet, you come to an intersection where the trail switchbacks to the left. Another quick switchback takes you to the creek crossing (13S0390709E, 4364831N, 10,140 feet). Continue on the somewhat steeply dropping Colorado Trail to the edge of a large open area where the Colorado Trail goes right and the 10ᵗʰ Mountain trail heads across the open area SW towards the road (usually snowmobile-packed) ahead. On reaching the road (13S0390488E, 4364213N, 9,610 feet) by a small wooden fence, take a left. Go ¼ mile up the road and watch carefully for a blue diamond on a tree on the right (13S0390762E, 4363988N, 9,585 feet) indicating the right turn off the road and across the East Fork drainage. Put on your skins, cross the drainage and follow the trail heading SW through the open area and up into the trees. The well-marked trail ascends for about 1½ miles through the trees to some switchbacks at 10,100 feet, continues through a flat area in the trees to an ascent in Jones Gulch.

At the top of the gulch the trail heads W to a large open area. Stay along the right edge of the open area, heading W to a rising traverse into the trees. Continue for about ½ mile on the well-marked trail to intersect the crest of the ridge (13S0387657E, 4363122N) at 10,670 feet. Take a left to follow the trail going up the ridge to a road intersection at 11,060 feet (13S038805E, 4362102N) and turn right. You can take off your skins and follow the road cut on a level traverse for .6 miles to a fork (13S0388043E, 4361125N), where the road goes right and a marked trail goes to the left. Head left on the trail on a traverse the last .7 miles to the hut at the bottom of a clearing, making sure not to drop down right on a road cut about 300 yards before the hut.

12.3 Jackal Hut to Fowler/Hilliard Hut

Difficulty: Intermediate/advanced
Distance: 7.8 miles
Time: 7-9 hours
Text Map: p. 96
10ᵗʰ Mtn Map: Chicago Ridge
USGS Map: Pando
Elevation Gain: 2,090 feet; loss: 2,220 feet

Notes: This route involves a fairly steep descent into the Pearl Creek drainage at the beginning, and a steep 1,800-foot climb from Resolution Road to get to Fowler/Hilliard at the end of the tour, so only well-conditioned skiers with advanced skiing skills should consider this route. Watch your map carefully to avoid missing the first turn that takes you down into the Pearl Creek drainage. On the approach to the Fowler/Hilliard avoid the temptation to drop down from the top of Resolution Mountain to the hut, as avalanche danger may exist in Resolution Bowl and on the open slopes of Resolution Mountain.

Route Description: From the Jackal Hut head E down the open area of the ridge .6 miles to a saddle at 11,420 feet (13S0390959E, 4366119N). Take the marked trail dropping down to the left (N) through the trees. Continue on the steep descent, following the left side of a small gully after dropping off a steep ridge, until you drop into the Pearl Creek drainage at 10,545 feet. Go left, staying along the left (S) side of the drainage on a trail, poorly marked at first, then very obvious, for 2.1 miles on a gradual descent to Resolution Road (13S0388208E, 4368638N, 9,690 feet). Go right up the wide Resolution Road for one mile (watch for snowmobiles) to a drainage on the left (13S0388654E, 4370116N, 9,960 feet) with a marked 10th Mountain route. Head left (ENE) up the gully, watch for the switchback up to the left out of the floor of the gully at 10,200 feet, and continue on the steep, switchbacking marked trail to a small saddle at 10,950 feet.

From the saddle ascend the ridge NE. At 11,360 feet (13S0388149E, 4371224N) stay straight as a trail drops off to the left toward McAllister Gulch. Continue up the ridge for about 100 yards past the intersection and then continue on a climbing traverse NNE and then N along the western face of Resolution Mountain. (Don't be tempted to follow the ridge to the top of Resolution Mountain, because then you'll have to descend the avalanche-prone eastern slope of Resolution Mountain to the hut.) At the saddle at 11,740 feet (Resolution Saddle, 13S0388457E, 4372062N) on the NW side of the mountain, turn right (E) and head on a ½-mile dropping traverse along the right side of the rocky formations of Resolution Narrows toward the hut which will be visible ahead in clear weather conditions.

A happy skier leaving the Jackal Hut after a good visit.

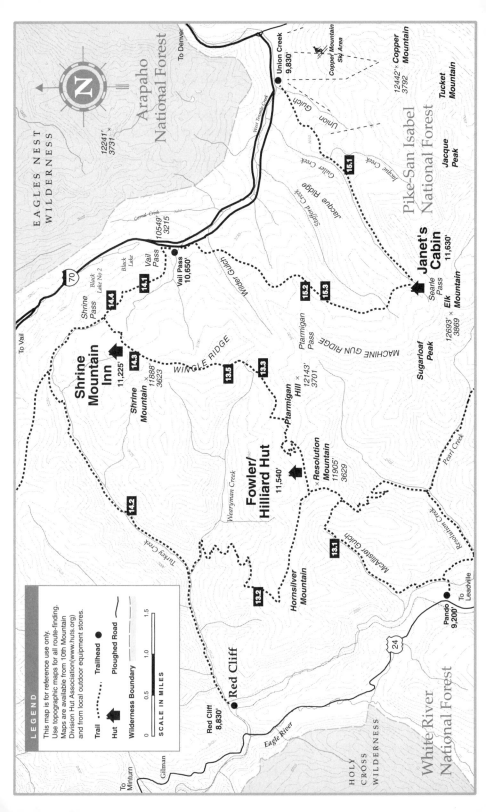

Chapter 13 • Fowler/Hilliard Hut

The Fowler/Hilliard Hut, built as a memorial to two Denver residents killed in a climbing accident near Aspen, is situated in one of the most spectacular settings of any hut in the 10th Mountain Hut System. Located on the shoulder of Resolution Mountain,

Elevation: 11,540 feet
Coordinates: 13S0389090E, 4372275N
County: Eagle
Access: I-70 at Vail Pass, Highway 24 at Camp Hale

the hut has marvelous views of the Elk Ridge and some of the highest peaks in Colorado. Skiing near the hut is great for all levels of skiers. The main attractions are the sometimes avalanche-prone Resolution Bowl, Ptarmigan Hill to the east, and the many open slopes and glades between the hut and Ptarmigan Hill. The easiest and most popular access to the hut is from the Pando Trailhead in Camp Hale. A longer route from Vail Pass is used by many skiers coming from the Denver area and can include an overnight stay in the Shrine Mountain Inn. The route to the hut from the Red Cliff Trailhead is the longest access and therefore not often used, but it includes a spectacular ridge route over Hornsilver Mountain. The hut can also be accessed via Resolution Creek from the Pando Trailhead, or the Camp Hale Trailhead (13S0385954E, 4365915N, 9,260 feet), although these routes involve more snowmobile traffic.

13.1 Pando Trailhead to Fowler/Hilliard Hut

Difficulty: Intermediate
Distance: 5 miles
Time: 4-6 hours
Text Map: pp. 96, 108
10ᵗʰ Mtn Map: Chicago Ridge
USGS Map: Pando
Elevation Gain: 2,500 feet: loss: 160 feet

Notes: This popular, direct route to the Fowler/Hilliard takes you from Camp Hale up McAllister Gulch to a high altitude beautiful traverse above timber line around Resolution Mountain to the hut. The last part of the route is quite steep and navigation can be somewhat tricky above timber line, so pay close attention to your map and compass. On the approach to the Fowler/Hilliard avoid the temptation to drop down from the top of Resolution Mountain to the hut, as avalanche danger may exist in Resolution Bowl and on the open slopes of Resolution Mountain.

Directions to Trailhead: From I-70 turn off at the Minturn exit (Exit 171) 5 miles west of Vail and go south for 15.6 miles to a road on the left just over a bridge at the beginning of the Camp Hale open area. Drive down the road about 150 yards to parking and the trailhead (13S0385619E, 4368082N, 9,200 feet).

From the intersection of highways 24 and 91 just north of Leadville, drive north on Highway 24 for 16.8 miles to the road and parking area for the Pando Trailhead on the right side of the road (.6 miles past the Snowmobile Rental Lodge with the Pando sign over the entrance). Note that this trailhead is a part of the Vail Pass Recreation Area and a parking fee is required. This fee is included in your fee for the hut, so carry a copy of your hut waiver to show you have paid.

Trailhead parking at the flats of Camp Hale.

Route Description: Head out of end of parking lot, cross the Eagle River on a snow bridge and go left (N) on the road on the other side of the river. Continue on the wide, road for one-half mile to the well-signed turn up Road 708 into McAllister Gulch on the right (13S0385588E, 4368943N, 9,250 feet). Put on your skins here if you haven't already done so. An angling traverse up the front side of the ridge will get you into the right side of McAllister Gulch where you start heading up steeply along the gulch in the pines.

The next two miles are a gradual climb up the right side of the gulch, until at 10,460 feet the route bends right (SE) and heads up steeply via switchbacks through the conifers to the top of the ridge at 11,360 feet (13S0388149E, 4371224N) where you have great views of the Elk Ridge to the east.

The route continues up the ridge to the left (NE) for about 100 yards and then continues on a climbing traverse NNE and then N along the western face of Resolution Mountain. (Don't be tempted to follow the ridge to the top of Resolution Mountain, because then you'll have to descend the avalanche-prone eastern slope of Resolution Mountain to the hut.) At the saddle at 11,740 feet (Resolution Saddle, 13S0388457E, 4372062N) on the NW side of the mountain, turn right (E) and head on a half-mile dropping traverse along the right side of the rocky formations of Resolution Narrows toward the hut which will be visible ahead in clear weather conditions.

Reverse Route: From the hut head WSW for one-half mile up through the rocky Resolution Narrows on the north side of Resolution Mountain to Resolution Saddle at 11,740 feet. Take a left (S) at the saddle and continue on a steady, slowly dropping traverse along the west side of Resolution Mountain through the open area until you gain the top of the ridge at a little over 11,400 feet. Follow the ridge to the trail going off to the right into the trees at 11,360 feet (13S0388149E, 4371224N). Head right (NW) down the steep, switchbacking trail through the conifers to a left (SW) turn at 10,460 feet which takes you on a steady 2-mile drop along the left side of McAllister Gulch.

As you near the bottom of the gulch and the flats of Camp Hale, the road turns to the SE and traverses down to the well-traveled wide road at the base of the mountain. Go left (S) for one-half mile to a right onto the track taking you across a snow bridge into the Pando parking area.

13.2 Red Cliff Trailhead to Fowler/Hilliard Hut

Difficulty: Intermediate/advanced
Distance: 7.9 miles (from the water tank)
Time: 8-11 hours up; 6-7 hours down
Text Map: pp. 96, 108
10ᵗʰ Mtn Map: Resolution Mountain
USGS Map: Red Cliff, Pando
Elevation Gain: 3,060 feet; loss: 350 feet

Notes: This long, but scenic, route via Hornsilver Mountain to the Fowler/Hilliard Hut from Red Cliff does not present too much difficulty in the way of route finding (except during bad weather above timber line), but the 3,000-foot steep climb can wear out the toughest of hutgoers, especially when trail has to be broken. This access is best used as part of a loop to Fowler/Hilliard, then to Shrine Mountain Inn, with a return down Shrine Pass Road. Shrine Pass Road and Wearyman Creek Road are frequently used by snowmobiles, which usually means a packed route, but some traffic. The Hornsilver Mountain summit offers a spectacular 360-degree view of the highest mountains in north central Colorado, and is worth the extra effort in using this route. Pay close attention to potential avalanche danger on the slopes of Resolution Mountain.

Directions to Trailhead: From I-70 take the Minturn Exit #171 (5 miles west of Vail) and go south on Highway 24 for 10.4 miles to the Red Cliff turnoff on the left. Go one mile down the road into Red Cliff and take the first left on Shrine Pass Road, which leads up into the Turkey Creek drainage. Drive 1.1 miles up the road to a large water tank on the right (13S0383857E, 4375281N, 8,830 feet) where you can park. If the road is not drivable, you may have to park in Red Cliff and ski the extra 1.1 miles up the road.

Route Description: From the water tank parking area, ski up the Shrine Pass Road for 1.4 miles to Wearyman Creek Road (FDR 747) on the right (13S0386070E, 4375721N, 9,060 feet). Turn right and follow Wearyman Creek Road for ¾ mile, crossing the creek 5 times. Immediately after the 5ᵗʰ crossing take a hard right onto the Hornsilver Mountain jeep trail which angles up to the right (WSW). Stay on the steep, switchbacking main road (marked by blue diamonds), avoiding side roads. At 10,870 feet (13S385678E, 4373852N), stay straight on the main road as a side road goes off to the right. In another 100 yards

112

stay straight again as another road goes off to the right. As the way starts opening up you will get onto Hornsilver Mountain Ridge (13S0385501E, 4373100N, 11,310 feet) and start heading SE up the ridge, through some trees at first, then in the open. Keep heading (ESE) along the ridge to the top of Hornsilver Mountain (13S0386147E, 4372813N, 11,615 feet), and enjoy the spectacular view.

Continue following the ridge slightly S of E, staying to the right of one small hillock with a few trees, and drop down to a large, wide open saddle (13S0387446E, 4372516N, 11,490 feet). Head due E up through the open area, watching for a marked trail angling up to the right through the trees (13S0387996E, 4372433N, 11,615 feet) beyond the saddle. Continue SE and into the open just before Resolution Mountain.

Here at Resolution Saddle (13S0388433E, 4372001N, 11,740 feet), watch your map, compass and altimeter very closely, and take care not to drop down too far to the left. Head very slightly north of E to enter a rock-walled gully (Resolution Narrows) up against Resolution Mountain. On a clear day you can see the hut ahead to the E. Follow the gut of the gully for a little less than ½ mile to the hut.

Reverse Route: From the hut head WSW for ½ mile up through the rocky Resolution Narrows on the north side of Resolution Mountain to Resolution Saddle at 11,740 feet. Go right on a NW bearing, following the marked route that drops down through patches of trees to an open area at 11,615 feet. Drop W to a large, open saddle (13S0387446E, 4372516N, 11,490 feet) and continue on a WNW bearing to the summit of Hornsilver Mountain.

Continue WNW down the ridge of Hornsilver Mountain, entering some trees at 11,450 feet (13S0385782E, 4372956N),and then leave the ridge at 11,310 feet to swing right and follow a NNE descent on the marked road cut, taking care not to turn left on two side roads at about 10,900 feet. Continue dropping on the obvious, marked Hornsilver Mountain jeep trail as it switchbacks down steeply to Wearyman Creek at 9,300 feet. Take a left to cross the creek and follow the Wearyman Creek Road down W and then NW as it crosses the creek four more times before reaching Turkey Creek at 9,060 feet. Cross Turkey Creek and take a left on Shrine Pass Road for the last 1.4 miles to the parking area by the water tank.

13.3 Vail Pass Trailhead to Fowler/Hilliard Hut

Difficulty: Intermediate/advanced
Distance: 9.5 miles
Time: 8-10 hours up; 7-8 hours down
Text Map: p. 108
10ᵗʰ Mtn Map: Resolution Mountain
USGS Map: Vail Pass, Red Cliff, Pando
Elevation Gain: 1,810 feet; loss: 920 feet

Notes: This trip to the Fowler/Hilliard Hut from Vail Pass follows the route to Shrine Mountain Inn and then goes via Shrine Mountain Ridge to the Fowler/Hilliard. The route is long and challenging, especially in bad weather conditions. Be well prepared with maps, a compass, altimeter, and a GPS, if possible, especially for the Shrine Mountain Ridge traverse. Under severe weather conditions, rethink making this trip, since you will be exposed to high winds and poor visibility on the ridge, which will make navigation extremely arduous and difficult. The last part of the trip involves a somewhat boring, gradual ascent up a snowmobile road.

Directions to Trailhead: Take I-70 for 14 miles east from Vail or 5 miles west from Copper Mountain Resort to exit 190 at Vail Pass. Park in the overnight parking lot on the right just after crossing over I-70 on the exit road. The user fee for the Vail Pass Recreation Area is included in your price for the hut, so have a copy of your 10ᵗʰ Mountain waiver form in your possession.

Route Description: Head up snowmobile-packed Shrine Pass Road going uphill just past the overnight parking entrance. About 150 yards up the road, at the first switchback, is the marked trailhead (13S0395146E, 4376137N, 10,650 feet) for the ski trail which takes off to the left. Do not go up Shrine Pass Road any further! Follow the well-marked and well-used trail on a gradual uphill on the right side of the West Tenmile Creek drainage for a little over 2 miles to the head of the drainage, where the trail veers to the left (W) to enter the trees (13S0393267E, 4378034N, 11,130 feet). Follow the rising road cut in the trees for the last ¼ mile (S) to the Shrine Mountain Inn.

Continue SW about one-quarter mile to Walter's Cabin and head on a SSW bearing on a marked trail through open area and scattered trees. In just less than a mile from the cabin, you will follow a gully and ascend a steep ridge on the left, just before the wide open Shrine Mountain Saddle (13S0392066E, 4376526N, 11,750 feet) on the left (S) side of the Shrine Mountain summit. From the saddle continue on a SSW bearing, traversing at about 11,700 feet below Shrine Mountain Ridge and

Part of the upstairs communal sleeping area in the Fowler/Hilliard Hut.

near timber line. Pay close attention to your map and compass as the route eventually turns SSE and drops to enter the trees at 11,525 feet (13S0392000E, 4374518N). The marked trail continues to drop through the trees SE and then S as the pitch gets very steep down an open hillside. At 11,120 feet turn W to go under some power lines and head steeply down into the open area to cross Wearyman Creek, just beyond which you pick up a road (13S0391908E, 4373921N, 11,040 feet). Head W and then SW on the well-traveled road for .2 miles on a downhill to a clearing on the right.

From here the road will be gradually climbing (skins aren't necessary if you have fish scales or a good wax) for 3 miles. One mile beyond the clearing (13S0390303E, 4373435N, 11,025 feet), at a road intersection, stay left to continue the climb on the main road. At the next road coming in from the right, stay straight on the main road. Then, after four long switchbacks, watch carefully for the road going off to the hut at 11,520 feet (13S0389459E, 4372504N) on the right, just before the hut boundary gates. Take this road as it loops around to the right through the 10th Mountain summer parking area and a gate, where you go SSW over a slight rise to the Fowler/Hilliard Hut.

Reverse Route: From the front of the Fowler/Hilliard Hut (skins aren't necessary) head ENE over a very slight rise and veer NNE through an open area onto the road. Follow the road through the gate and 10th Mountain summer parking area, and left to the hut boundary gates. Just past the gates, at the junction with the Ptarmigan Hill Road

(13S0389459E, 4372504N, 11,520 feet), go left (NE) as the wide road gently switchbacks down. After 4 switchbacks, at 11,100 feet, go straight as a road comes in from the left. Next, bear right as another road comes in from the left (13S0390303E, 4373435N, 11,025 feet). In another mile, the road bottoms out by a clearing on the left (13S0391738E, 4373610N, 10,875 feet). Put on your skins here and climb .2 miles up the road to a large open area at the head of Wearyman Creek. Watch carefully as the route leaves the road (13S0391908E, 4373921N, 11,040 feet) and heads E to cross Wearyman Creek.

Beyond the creek go up steeply under some power lines and take an immediate left (N) to follow the very steep trail up through a small open hillside and into the trees. Watch your map and compass carefully here as the trail heads first N, then NW through the trees. At 11,525 feet (13S0392000E, 4374518N) the route enters the wide open flank of Shrine Mountain Ridge. From here on, you may have to rely on your map, compass and altimeter to get to Shrine Mountain Saddle, since at and above timber line there are very few blue diamonds. Climb NNW to 11,680 feet and continue on a traverse (staying around 11,700 feet) that slowly takes you to a NNE bearing toward the Shrine Mountain Saddle (13S0392066E, 4376526N, 11,750 feet) on the SE edge of Shrine Mountain.

On the other side of the saddle, pick up the marked trail that goes off to the left along a small ridge above a gully on the left. Drop down the ridge, following the blue diamonds on the safest route into the gully. Follow the trail through the gully and then continue on a NNE bearing through scattered trees, taking care not to drop right into the large open drainage. In about one mile from the saddle you will enter an open area and see Walter's Cabin (13S0392775E, 4377665N, 11,260 feet) ahead. Go to the right of Walter's and head NE for about .2 miles, and pick up the road cut in front of the Shrine Mountain Inn that that heads N through the trees toward Shrine Pass.

As the route exits into the open area at the head of the West Tenmile Creek, take the trail going E and follow the marked ski trail as it gradually drops SE along the left side of the drainage for just over 2 miles to the trailhead. Go right down Shrine Pass Road for the last 150 yards to the parking area.

13.4 Fowler/Hilliard Hut to Jackal Hut

Difficulty: Intermediate/advanced
Distance: 7.8 miles
Time: 7-9 hours
Text Map: p. 96
10ᵗʰ Mtn Map: Chicago Ridge
USGS Map: Pando
Elevation Gain: 2,220 feet; loss: 2,090 feet

Notes: This popular route between these two huts avoids snowmobile traffic except for the one mile on Resolution Road, making this a very pleasant backcountry hut-to-hut trip. However, the length of the trip, the steep initial descent to Resolution Road, and the steep ascent from Pearl Creek to the hut make this a demanding trip for intermediate skiers and those not well acclimated to the altitude. The sections above timber line and the exit from the Pearl Creek drainage can involve some route-finding skills, so pay close attention to navigation. Experienced, advanced skiers can try the shortcut down Resolution Bowl from the hut to Resolution Road to save some time and get in some turns. Be aware that avalanche danger exists in Resolution Bowl and on the open slopes of Resolution Mountain.

Avalanche-prone Resolution Mountain as seen from the Fowler/Hilliard Hut.

Route Description: From the hut head WSW for ½ mile up through the rocky Resolution Narrows on the north side of Resolution Mountain to Resolution Saddle at 11,740 feet (13S0388457E, 4372062N). Take a left (S) at the saddle and continue on a steady, slowly dropping traverse along the west side of Resolution Mountain through the open area until you gain the top of the ridge at a little over 11,400 feet. Continue down along the ridge into the trees (do not drop down on the trail going off to the right at 11,360 feet). Follow the ridge SW on a steady, well-marked dropping trail through the trees, to a small saddle at 10,950 feet. From here head left and continue down along a gully via steep switchbacks.

The SE-facing slopes can have some cruddy snow at times, so use caution, especially as the trail narrows through the trees. In good snow, the switchbacks can be cut with a few good turns. Continue descending along the right side of the drainage, dropping to the creek at 10,200 feet and following the gully to the intersection with Resolution Road (13S0388654E, 4370116N, 9,960 feet). Go right (S) one mile down the wide Resolution Road to the Pearl Creek drainage on the left.

Just past Pearl Creek turn onto Road 715 (13S0388208E, 4368638N, 9,690 feet) for about 100 feet and pick up the 10th Mountain trail going off to the left along the south side of Pearl Creek. Put on your skins and follow the obvious trail up along the right side of the Pearl Creek drainage for 2 miles. Just as the drainage turns left (NE) at 10,545 feet go right (SSE) up through an open area. This turn (13S0391210E, 4367349N) may not be well marked, so watch the map and your navigation instruments carefully.

Continue up the right side of a small gully. The marked route soon climbs quite steeply up a ridge and then continues S up through the woods to a saddle at 11,420 feet (13S0390959E, 4366119N) with great views over the other side. At the saddle take a right (W) to make a gradual ascent along a ridge for .6 miles to the 10th Mountain summer parking area where you drop down a couple of hundred feet to the hut just below the summit. Sometimes a track traverses through the open area on the south face of the ridge directly to the Jackal Hut (13S0390054E, 4366191N, 11,670 feet), thus avoiding the extra climb to the summit.

13.5 Fowler/Hilliard Hut to Shrine Mountain Inn

Difficulty: Intermediate/advanced
Distance: 6.8 miles
Time: 6-7 hours
Text Map: p. 108
10th Mtn Map: Resolution Mountain
USGS Map: Pando, Red Cliff, Vail Pass
Elevation Gain: 920 feet; loss: 1,235 feet

Notes: This hut-to-hut route, although not as physically demanding as some hut-to-hut routes, involves a few navigational challenges, especially in bad weather conditions. Be well prepared with maps, a compass, altimeter, and a GPS, if possible, especially for the Shrine

Mountain Ridge traverse. Under severe weather conditions, rethink making this trip, since you will be exposed to high winds and poor visibility on the ridge, making navigation arduous and difficult.

Route Description: From the front of the hut (skins aren't necessary) head ENE over a very slight rise and veer NNE through an open area onto the road. Follow the road through the gate and 10th Mountain summer parking area, beyond which it loops back to the left. Just beyond the hut boundary gates, at the junction with the Ptarmigan Hill Road (13S0389459E, 4372504N, 11,520 feet), go left (NE) as the wide road gently switchbacks down. After 4 switchbacks, at 11,100 feet, go straight as a road comes in from the left. Next, bear right as another road comes in from the left (13S0390303E, 4373435N, 11,025 feet). In another mile, the road bottoms out by a clearing on the left (13S0391738E, 4373610N, 10,875 feet).

Put on your skins here and climb .2 miles up the road to a large open area at the head of Wearyman Creek. Watch carefully as the route leaves the road (13S0391908E, 4373921N, 11,040 feet) and heads E to cross Wearyman Creek. Beyond the creek go up steeply under some power lines and take an immediate left (N) to follow the very steep trail up through a small open hillside and into the trees. Watch your map and compass carefully here as the trail heads first N, then NW through the trees. At 11,525 feet (13S0392000E, 4374518N) the route enters the wide open flank of Shrine Mountain Ridge. From here on, you may have to rely on your map, compass and altimeter to get to Shrine Mountain Saddle, since at and above timber line there are very few blue diamonds. Climb NNW to 11,680 feet and continue on a traverse (staying around 11,700 feet) that slowly takes you to a NNE bearing toward the Shrine Mountain Saddle (13S0392066E, 4376526N, 11,750 feet) on the SE edge of Shrine Mountain.

On the other side of the saddle, pick up the marked trail that goes off to the left along a small ridge above a gully on the left. Drop down the ridge, following the blue diamonds on the safest route into the gully. Follow the trail through the gully and then continue on a NNE bearing through scattered trees, taking care not to drop right into the large open drainage. In about one mile from the saddle you will enter an open area and see Walter's Cabin (13S0392775E, 4377665N, 11,260 feet) ahead. To get to Jay's and Chuck's Cabin, go to the right of Walter's and head NE for about .2 miles.

Chapter 14 • **Shrine Mountain Inn**

The privately owned Shrine Mountain Inn actually consists of the original Inn (Jay's), and two large cabins (Chuck's and Walter's) with room for separate groups both upstairs and downstairs. The cabins are ideal

Elevation: 11,225 feet (Jay's)
Coordinates: 13S0393022E, 4377860N
County: Eagle
Access: I-70 at Vail Pass

for families, and Walter's (about a quarter mile SW of Jay's) boasts a good hill for sledding. A detached sauna is available close to Jay's and Chuck's. Running water and showers make the Shrine Mountain Inn one of luxury stops for hutgoers.

Ski touring in the area of the huts is plentiful; those looking for turns should head up to nearby Shrine Mountain. The access from Vail Pass is the shortest and easiest to any hut in the 10th Mountain Hut System, helping make these huts quite popular all times of the year. The longer access from Red Cliff is usually just used as part of a longer loop involving the Fowler/Hilliard Hut.

14.1 Vail Pass Trailhead to Shrine Mountain Inn

Difficulty: Beginner
Distance: 2.7 miles
Time: 2 hours up; 1 hour down
Text Map: p. 108
10ᵗʰ Mtn Map: Resolution Mountain
USGS Map: Vail Pass
Elevation Gain: 575 feet

Notes: The route to the Shrine Mountain Inn, which formerly followed Shrine Pass Road, now follows a ski trail to keep away from snowmobile traffic. The ski trail is marked by poles and by blue diamonds and is mostly in the open, so be prepared for high winds and poor visibility in inclement weather. The user fee for the Vail Pass Recreation Area is included in your price for the hut, so have a copy of your 10ᵗʰ Mountain waiver form in your possession.

Directions to Trailhead: Take I-70 14 miles east from Vail or 5 miles west from Copper Mountain Resort to Exit 190 at Vail Pass. Park in the overnight parking lot on the right just after the exit road crosses I-70.

Route Description: Head up snowmobile-packed Shrine Pass Road just past the overnight parking entrance. About 150 yards up the road, at the first switchback, is the marked trailhead (13S0395146E, 4376137N, 10,650 feet) for the ski trail which takes off to the left. Do not go up Shrine Pass Road any further! Follow the well-marked and well-used trail on a gradual uphill up the right side of the West Tenmile Creek drainage for a little over 2 miles up to the head of the drainage, where the trail veers to the left (W) to enter the trees (13S0393267E, 4378034N, 11,130 feet). Follow the rising road cut in the trees for the last ¼ mile (S) to the Shrine Mountain Inn.

Reverse Route: From the Shrine Mountain Inn (Jay's) follow the road cut that heads N through the trees toward Shrine Pass. As it exits into the open area at the head of the West Tenmile Creek, take the trail going E and follow the marked ski trail as it gradually drops SE along the left side of the drainage for just over 2 miles to the trailhead. Go right down Shrine Pass Road for the last 150 yards to the parking area.

14.2 Red Cliff Trailhead to Shrine Mountain Inn

Difficulty: Beginner/intermediate
Distance: 8.2 miles (from water tank)
Time: 6-7 hours up; 3-5 hours down
Text Map: p. 108
10ᵗʰ Mtn Map: Resolution Mountain
USGS Map: Red Cliff, Vail Pass
Elevation Gain: 2,395 feet

Notes: This well-used, long, gentle route via Shrine Pass Road up the Turkey Creek drainage is frequented by snowmobiles and is therefore usually well packed. Route finding is not much of a problem, except that snowmobile tracks veering off to the side can cause confusion. Also, care must be taken at Shrine Pass to not miss the right turn to the hut. This route is mainly used for those making a loop from Red Cliff to Shrine Mountain Inn, Fowler/Hilliard via Shrine Mountain Ridge, and back to Red Cliff via Hornsilver Mountain. Almost all hutgoers heading just to the Shrine Mountain Inn use the short and easy route from Vail Pass.

Directions to Trailhead: From I-70 take the Minturn Exit #171 (5 miles west of Vail) and go south on Highway 24 for 10.4 miles to the Red Cliff turnoff on the left. Go one mile down the road into Red Cliff and take the first left on Shrine Pass Road which leads up into the Turkey Creek drainage. Drive 1.1 miles up the road to a large water tank on the right (13S0383857E, 4375281N, 8,830 feet) where you can park. If the road is not drivable, you may have to park in Red Cliff and ski the extra 1.1 miles up the road.

Route Description: From the water tank parking area, ski up the Shrine Pass Road for 1.4 miles, where you pass Wearyman Creek Road (FDR 747) which goes off to the right. Continue straight on the obvious Shrine Pass Road as it crosses the creek in about 200 feet, continues on a gradual climb through the trees and recrosses the creek at 9,630 feet, just after passing the remains of a couple of old log cabins. At 10,400 feet (13S0391040E, 4379380N), where Road 713 goes up to the right across the creek, stay left on Shrine Pass Road as it switchbacks left then right and continues NE to the well-signed intersection with Lime Creek Road 728 at 10,700 feet (13S0391880E, 4379729N). Go right (SE) to stay in the Turkey Creek drainage on Shrine Pass Road, with the road soon crossing the creek in a large clearing at 10,895 feet

(13S0392886E, 4379174N) and then entering the trees. Continue up along the left side of the drainage through the open area until you come to some signs at 11,120 feet (13S0393321E, 4378112N) in the middle of the large open area at Shrine Pass. Go SW 200 feet toward a road cut entering the trees (13S0393267E, 4378034N, 11,130 feet) and follow the rising road cut (S) the last ¼ mile to the Shrine Mountain Inn.

Reverse Route: From the Shrine Mountain Inn (Jay's) go SE from the front of the cabin and bear left to follow the road cut that heads N through the trees toward Shrine Pass. As it exits into the open area at the head of the West Tenmile Creek, go straight (NE) for about 200 feet toward

Walter's Cabin.

some signs (13S0393321E, 4378112N, 11,120 feet) and then bear left onto Shrine Pass Road which goes left down along the right side of Turkey Creek drainage. Pay close attention as the road passes through the open and then some trees before crossing the creek at 10,895 feet (13S0392886E, 4379174N) in a large clearing.

At the well-signed intersection with Lime Creek Road 728 (13S0391880E, 4379729N, 10,700 feet), stay on Road 709 going down to the left. In another one-half mile, after taking a switchback to the left, avoid crossing the creek onto Road 713 going uphill. Stay right on Shrine Pass Road (13S0391040E, 4379380N, 10,400 feet) to continue down (WSW) along the right side of Turkey Creek. As the drainage narrows, the road continues to drop steadily to another creek crossing at 9,630 feet. Just beyond the crossing are the remains of a couple of old cabins on the left.

The next creek crossing is just before the Wearyman Creek turnoff. About 200 feet beyond the crossing a sign indicates Red Cliff straight ahead and Wearyman Creek Road (FDR 747) to the left (13S0386070E, 4375721N, 9,060 feet). Continue straight along the right side of the creek for the last 1.4 miles to the trailhead at the water tank.

14.3 Shrine Mountain Inn to Fowler/Hilliard Hut

Difficulty: Intermediate/advanced
Distance: 6.8 miles
Time: 6-8 hours
Text Map: p. 108
10ᵗʰ Mtn Map: Resolution Mountain
USGS Map: Pando, Red Cliff, Vail Pass
Elevation Gain: 1,235 feet; loss: 920 feet

Notes: This hut-to-hut route, although not as physically demanding as some hut-to-hut routes, involves a few navigational challenges, especially in bad weather conditions. Be well prepared with maps, a compass, altimeter, and a GPS, if possible, especially for the Shrine Mountain Ridge traverse. Under severe weather conditions, rethink making this trip, since you will be exposed to high winds and poor visibility on the ridge, which will make navigation extremely arduous and difficult. The last part of the trip involves a somewhat boring gradual ascent up a snowmobile road.

Route Description: From Jay's/Chuck's Cabin head SW about ¼ mile to Walter's Cabin and continue from Walter's on a SSW bearing on a marked trail through open area and scattered trees on a gradual ascent toward the saddle on the left (S) side of the Shrine Mountain summit. In a little less than a mile from the cabin, you will enter a gully which you follow, ascending a steep ridge on the left, just before the saddle. From the wide open Shrine Mountain Saddle (13S0392066E, 4376526N, 11,750 feet) follow a SSW bearing, traversing at about 11,700 feet below Shrine Mountain Ridge and near timber line. Pay close attention to your map and compass as the route eventually turns SSE and drops to enter the trees at 11,525 feet (13S0392000E, 4374518N).

Chuck's Cabin

The marked trail continues to drop SE through the trees and then S as the pitch gets very steep down an open hillside. At 11,120 feet turn W to go under some power lines and head steeply down into the open area to cross Wearyman Creek, just beyond which you pick up a road (13S0391908E, 4373921N, 11,040 feet). Head W and then SW on the well-traveled road for .2 miles on a downhill to a clearing on the right. From here the road gradually climbs (skins aren't necessary if you have fish scales or a good wax) for 3 miles.

One mile beyond the clearing (13S0390303E, 4373435N, 11,025 feet), at a road intersection, stay left to continue the climb on the main road. In just under a mile, at the next road coming in from the right, stay straight on the main road. Then, after four long switchbacks, watch carefully for the road going off to the hut at 11,520 feet (13S0389459E, 4372504N) on the right, just before the hut boundary gates. Take this road as it loops around to the right through the 10th Mountain summer parking area and a gate, where you go SSW over a slight rise to the hut.

14.4 Shrine Mountain Inn to Janet's Cabin

Difficulty: Advanced
Distance: 8.4 miles
Time: 6-8 hours
Text Map: p. 108
10th Mtn Map: Resolution Mountain
USGS Map: Vail Pass, Copper Mountain
Elevation Gain: 1,390 feet; loss: 985 feet

Notes: This hut-to-hut route between Shrine Mountain Inn and Janet's Cabin is seldom used, except on long ski-throughs. Expect to have to break trail from Vail Pass to Janet's Cabin. Good navigational skills are a must; have a compass, altimeter, and good maps. A GPS can also be very valuable, especially in bad weather when visibility is poor. The route is very scenic, but also very susceptible to blowing snow and poor visibility during storms. The route between Vail Pass and Janet's Cabin is mostly above timberline and is exposed to avalanche danger, especially below Machine Gun Ridge. Following the marked route in the trees (sometimes hard to find) during periods of high avalanche hazard can help avoid the slide danger.

Route Description: From the Shrine Mountain Inn (Jay's), follow the road cut that heads N through the trees toward Shrine Pass. As it exits into the open area at the head of the West Tenmile Creek, take the trail going E and follow the marked ski trail as it gradually drops SE along the left side of the drainage for just over 2 miles to the ski trailhead at Shrine Pass Road. Head S above the Vail Pass Rest Area parking toward the wide packed track which crosses the West Tenmile Creek drainage (13S0395175E, 4375975N, 10,600 feet) and continues parallel to I-70, traversing about one-half mile to Wilder Gulch. Cross the creek and stay to the right of a knob on the other side of the creek. Put on your skins if you haven't already done so.

From here you will ascend the broad ridge directly ahead and follow the ridgeline in a SSW direction. At 11,360 feet (13S0394321E, 4373547N) watch for a small clearing on the left (about 200 yards before the ridge rises up steeply). Leave the ridgeline, traverse across the steeply sloped clearing to drop into Smith Gulch. After the 70-foot vertical drop into Smith Gulch, the route follows the gulch through the trees to an open bowl. Stay along the left side of the bowl by the trees, as you head SE then S to 11,600 feet. Do not drop down into Stafford Creek drainage as you take a long southerly traverse around the head of the drainage, heading S and staying at around 11,600 feet, with Machine Gun Ridge off to the right.

Above timber line on the way to Janet's Cabin.

The marked trail moves in and out of the trees to avoid avalanche danger, but in times of low avalanche danger you may wish to stay just above the trees. Watch your map and altimeter closely as you climb above the drainage and start circling east, reaching an elevation of 11,680 feet. In your final approach to the hut, head SE to keep from dropping into Guller Creek drainage, until you spot Janet's Cabin right below you at the top of the drainage, surrounded by a few trees at timber line.

Chapter 15 • **Janet's Cabin**

The spacious Janet's Cabin, owned by the Summit Huts Association, is a popular destination for Denver and Front Range hutgoers, due largely to its convenient access, its first-class construction, and the wonderful sauna. Janet's Cabin is usually accessed via the shorter, easier route from Copper Mountain Resort, but advanced skiers and navigators can enjoy the route from Vail Pass which takes the hutgoer into the high country above timber line for most of the route.

Elevation: 11,630 feet
Coordinates: 13S0394173E, 4368998N
County: Summit
Access: I-70, Vail Pass/ Copper Mountain

Skiing opportunities near the hut are plentiful for all levels of skiers. The hut's timberline location allows for skiing in the trees below the hut, and for intermediate and advanced skiing in the bowls and on the ridge above the hut, especially on Sugarloaf Peak and Elk Mountain, and near Searle Pass. During World War II the 10th Mountain Division ski troops used these areas for their winter training. Be aware of avalanche danger in this steep terrain above timber line.

15.1 Union Creek Trailhead to Janet's Cabin

Difficulty: Beginner/intermediate
Distance: 4.6 miles
Time: 4-5 hours up; 2-3 hours down
Text Map: p. 108
10ᵗʰ Mtn Map: Resolution Mountain
USGS Map: Copper Mountain
Elevation Gain: 1,800 feet

Notes: The standard route from Copper Mountain Resort to Janet's Cabin up the Guller Creek drainage is the easiest and fastest way to get to the hut. Using the ski lifts can even shorten the route. The only potential avalanche danger is on the slope above the junction of Guller and Jacque creeks.

Directions to Trailhead: From I-70, 5 miles west of Vail Pass, turn S on Highway 91 and turn right into the main Copper Mountain Resort entrance. Take your first left into a parking area marked for Janet's Cabin and permit parking. Go left into the designated Janet's Cabin parking spaces. This area is in the north end of the Alpine lots near the Transportation Center, but must be accessed as described above. Post a copy of your parking permit from 10ᵗʰ Mountain in each car of your group and catch the shuttle bus from the Transportation Center to Union Creek. You cannot park at Union Creek.

Route Description: From the Union Creek base area (13S0399945E, 4372836N, 9,830 feet) you have two choices to get to the trail which leaves the ski area:

(1) Show your hut confirmation to the ticket window and get a one-ride pass for the lifts. Take the K and the L lifts. At the top of the L lifts go right off the lift and ski down on the far left (W) side of the ski area about one-quarter mile to 10,675 feet to a backcountry access point (13S0398379E, 4371958N) on the left side of the trail in the trees. The trail will be signed and marked by a blue diamond.

(2) From the Union Creek base area walk up the right side of the ski trails for about 800 vertical feet to 10,675 feet and the signed backcountry access point in the trees on the right.

From the backcountry access point, follow the marked trail through the trees as it descends about 200 feet to a small bridge crossing Guller

Creek at 10,465 feet. From here the marked trail takes a gradual climb up the right side of the drainage to 11,080 feet where it crosses to the left side of the creek. The trail stays above the drainage on the left, gradually climbing at first, and then more steeply right before the hut, to 11,630 feet and Janet's Cabin on the right side of the top of the drainage at timber line.

Reverse Route: From the cabin, cross over to the right (E) side of the Guller Creek drainage. The first section going down is the steepest, and some turns can be taken before the slope eases. Stay on the right as the slope of the descent quickly mellows out. After a drop of 500 feet in elevation, the trail crosses to the other (left) side of the drainage, first climbing into a few trees, then continuing on a gradual descent down the drainage. At 10,465 feet the trail again crosses the creek over a small bridge (13S0397616E, 4371604N) and then climbs, following the Colorado Trail for a while, about 200 vertical feet through the trees. The trail breaks out of the trees at a backcountry access point (13S0398379E, 4371958N, 10,675 feet) onto a Copper Mountain ski trail which can then be skied on the left side as it drops just over 800 vertical feet to the Union Creek base area and trailhead. From here a shuttle bus can be caught to the parking area at the Alpine lots where Janet's Cabin overnight parking is located.

15.2 Vail Pass Trailhead to Janet's Cabin

Difficulty: Advanced
Distance: 5.7 miles
Time: 5-7 hours up; 4-5 hours down
Text Map: p. 108
10th Mtn Map: Resolution Mountain
USGS Map: Vail Pass, Copper Mountain
Elevation Gain: 1,390 feet; loss: 410 feet

Notes: This beautiful, high-altitude route to Janet's Cabin is not used very much, so expect to have to break trail all or most of the way. Most of the route is above timber line, although the recommended route tries to stay in the trees when possible. Following the marked route in the trees (sometimes hard to find) during periods of high avalanche hazard can help avoid the slide danger below Machine Gun Ridge. Good navigational skills are a must; have a compass, altimeter, and good maps. A GPS can also be very valuable, especially in bad weather when visibility is poor during storms and periods of blowing snow. If you do have good navigational skills and good weather, take this route and enjoy the high country below Machine Gun Ridge near the hut. This entire area along this ridge was a winter training ground for the 10th Mountain Division ski troops during World War II. Note that this trailhead is a part of the Vail Pass Recreation Area and a use fee is required. This fee is included in your fee for the hut, so carry a copy of your hut waiver form to show that you have paid.

Directions to Trailhead: Take I-70 14 miles east from Vail or 5 miles west from Copper Mountain Resort to exit 190 at Vail Pass. Park in overnight parking on the right just after crossing over I-70. Walk down through the Rest Area Parking to access the trail which crosses the West Tenmile Creek drainage (13S0395175E, 4375975N, 10,600 feet).

Route Description: From the trailhead head SSE on the wide track (packed for snowmobiles) crossing the drainage and continuing parallel to I-70, traversing about ½ mile to Wilder Gulch. Cross the creek and stay to the right of a knob on the other side of the creek. Put on your skins if you haven't already done so. From here you will ascend the broad ridge directly ahead and follow the ridgeline in a SSW direction. At 11,360 feet (13S0394321E, 4373547N) watch for a small clearing on the left (about 200 yards before the ridge rises up steeply). Leave the ridgeline, traverse across the steeply sloped clearing to drop into Smith Gulch. After the 70-foot vertical drop into Smith Gulch, the route follows the gulch through the trees to an open bowl. Stay along the left side of the bowl by the trees, as you head SE then S to 11,600 feet. Do not drop down into Stafford Creek drainage as you take a long southerly traverse around the head of the drainage, heading S and staying at

Machine Gun Ridge and Sugarloaf Peak on the way to Janet's from Vail Pass.

around 11,600 feet, with Machine Gun Ridge off to the right. The marked trail moves in and out of the trees to avoid avalanche danger, but in times of low avalanche danger you may wish to stay just above the trees. Watch your map and altimeter closely as you climb above the drainage and start circling east, reaching an elevation of 11,680 feet. In your final approach to the hut, head SE to keep from dropping into Guller Creek drainage, until you spot Janet's Cabin right below you at the top of the drainage, surrounded by a few trees at timber line.

Reverse Route: Start by climbing NW up from the hut and follow a contour NW above the Stafford Creek drainages, dropping no lower than 11,600 feet and staying above timber line. Past the head of the Stafford Creek drainages, curve to the N and follow timber line at about 11,600 feet, until you rise over a ridge at 11,700 feet. Drop NW to a bowl which takes you NNE into the trees in Smith Gulch for a couple hundred yards to a rising traverse on the left up to the peak of the ridge. Follow the ridgeline NNE to the descent into Wilder Gulch. Cross the gulch and follow the main track as it traverses, paralleling I-70, to the parking area across West Tenmile Creek at Vail Pass.

15.3 Janet's Cabin to Shrine Mountain Inn

Difficulty: Advanced
Distance: 8.4 miles
Time: 7 hours
Text Map: p. 108
10ᵗʰ Mtn Map: Resolution Mountain
USGS Map: Vail Pass, Copper Mountain
Elevation Gain: 985 feet; loss: 1,390 feet

Notes: The part of this route from Janet's Cabin to Vail Pass below Machine Gun Ridge gets little use, is not well marked, and is above timber line, so good navigational skills are a must. In bad weather blowing snow and poor visibility can turn a pleasant trip into a navigational disaster. The route is also exposed to avalanche danger, especially below Machine Gun Ridge. Following the marked route in the trees (sometimes hard to find) during periods of high avalanche hazard can help avoid the slide danger. After the initial traverse, good turns can be made on the descent to Vail Pass. The last 2.7 miles from the Vail Pass area to the Shrine Mountain Inn are mellow in comparison, but care must still be taken as this section is also in the open.

Route Description: Start by climbing NW up from the hut and follow a contour NW above the Stafford Creek drainages, dropping no lower than 11,600 feet and staying above timber line. Past the head of the Stafford Creek drainages, curve to the N and follow timber line at about 11,600 feet, until you rise over a ridge at 11,700 feet. Drop NW to a bowl which takes you NNE into the trees in Smith Gulch for a couple hundred yards to a rising traverse on the left up to the peak of the ridge. Follow the ridgeline NNE to the descent into Wilder Gulch. Cross the gulch and follow the main track as it traverses, paralleling I-70, toward the parking area across West Tenmile Creek at Vail Pass. Stay above the parking area (put on your skins), and head up left about 100 yards on the snowmobile-packed Shrine Pass Road to the first switchback in the road, where the marked trailhead (13S0395146E, 4376137N, 10,650 feet) for the ski trail takes off to the left. Follow the well-marked and well-used trail on a gradual uphill up the right side of the West Tenmile Creek drainage for a little over 2 miles up to the head of the drainage where the trail veers to the left (W) to enter the trees (13S0393267E, 4378034N, 11,130 feet). Follow the rising road cut in the trees for the last one-quarter mile (S) to the Shrine Mountain Inn.

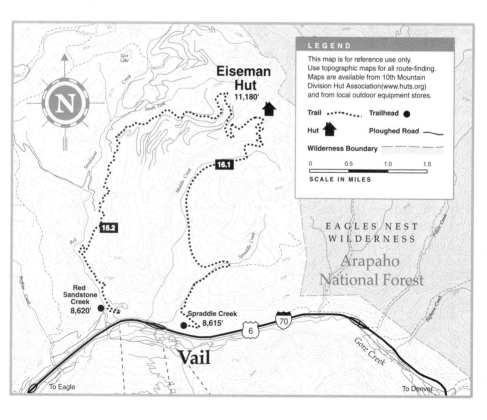

Chapter 16 • Eiseman Hut

The Eiseman Hut is one of the most popular huts in the 10th Mountain Hut System for many good reasons. The trailheads are very accessible, situated just off I-70 by Vail. The hut also offers probably the best skiing of

Elevation: 11,180 feet
Coordinates: 13S0384084E, 4394896N
County: Eagle
Access: I-70 at Vail.

any of the huts in the system. One can go in almost any direction from the hut and find outstanding intermediate and advanced skiing. And the views of the surrounding mountains are spectacular! On top of all this the Eiseman Hut is very spacious, with an elongated front to better enjoy the views of the peaks of the Gore Range.

The two trails leading to the hut offer the hutgoer a good choice. The Red Sandstone Creek route follows a road, and rises at a gentle grade, making it an easy trip for a novice skier. However, it is long and is used heavily by snowmobiles. The Spraddle Creek route, a more efficient route, is mostly trail, but goes up quite a bit steeper. It certainly is quieter and more pleasant as it rises through wooded areas, but it also can be a difficult downhill return for less advanced skiers. For good skiers, the downhill on this route offers great turns under good snow conditions. The ideal compromise for most is to use a car shuttle and go up the steeper Spraddle Creek route and return via the gentler Red Sandstone Creek route.

16.1 Spraddle Creek Trailhead to Eiseman Hut

Difficulty: Intermediate (Intermediate/advanced on the downhill)
Distance: 6.8 miles
Time: 5-7 hours up; 3-4 hours down
Text Map: p. 132
10th Mtn Map: Gore Range
USGS Map: Vail East
Elevation Gain: 2,845 feet; loss: 280 feet

Notes: This is the most direct, efficient, and pleasant route to the hut, but requires advanced skiing skills for the return downhill trip through the steeper, narrower sections. The route follows trail virtually the entire way, and route finding can take some time when the trail is not tracked out. Be aware that side tracks may veer from the trail.

Directions to Trailhead: Take I-70 to the main Vail exit (Exit 176), go to the North Frontage Road just north of the I-70 bridge and go right (E) where the sign indicates the turn to the Spraddle Creek Trailhead. Immediately on your left is the overflow parking area which can be used if all parking above is filled. Continue for .7 miles up the road to the entrance gate to the Spraddle Creek Estates. Do not park here, but take a very sharp right up onto a narrow road going steeply up the hill (4-wheel drive may be needed for this short hill) which leads to a small parking area at the trailhead (13S0382681E, 4389169N, 8,615 feet). There is only room for about 7 cars here, so carpool from the overflow parking area if your group has more than one car.

Route Description: Follow the road cut out of the back of the small parking area as it slowly climbs via a traverse to the Spraddle Creek drainage. You may be able to do the initial part of this route without skins, but you will need the skins eventually. Continue above Spraddle Creek for about 1½ miles until you come to an intersection at 9,565 feet (13S0383393E, 4390679N) where the road cut continues straight, but the trail angles off slightly to the left toward the creek. Follow the marked trail left to the creek crossing, following the trail on the other side as it cuts up sharply to the left (W) in the aspen trees. In less than one-half mile you will reach a clearing as the trail tops out at about 9,700 feet. Pay close attention to the route and your map here.

The trail initially drops a little WSW through the clearing into a larger lower clearing where you have to take a sharp right (N) into the trees (watch for the marked trail). The trail continues on a narrow downhill traverse into the Middle Creek drainage and then starts on a gradual uphill through beautiful stands of fir and spruce. After a little over 2 miles in the drainage the trail comes to the base of a steep small clearing at 10,600 feet (13S0384425E, 4394295N) where the serious climbing begins. After very steep switchbacks through the clearing, the fairly well-marked trail continues switchbacking up through the trees for the last mile until it breaks out of the woods and the Gore Range and the Vail Ski Area are visible ahead to the south as you drop a few feet to the hut.

The spacious interior of the Eiseman Hut.

Reverse Route:
From the Eiseman Hut go up (SE) a slight rise behind the hut on the marked trail into the trees and follow the downhill traverses and switchbacks first E, then S through the trees for a little over a mile into the Middle Creek drainage at 10,600 feet. From here the steepness eases as you follow the marked trail in the drainage to 9,500 feet where you start a climb S to a clearing at 9,700 feet. Head left (E) in the clearing on a slight ascent, and then continue E, soon dropping steeply on a narrow trail through the aspen to a crossing of Spraddle Creek. Take a right (SW) across the creek as the trail traverses to meet the jeep trail at 9,565 feet. Go straight (SW) and follow this road cut above Spraddle Creek to a SE traverse and then the final W traverse to the trailhead.

16.2 Red Sandstone Creek Trailhead to Eiseman Hut

Difficulty: Novice/intermediate
Distance: 8.7 miles (from road closure)
Time: 6-8 hours up; 3-4 hours down
Text Map: p. 132
10th Mtn Map: Gore Range
USGS Map: Vail East, Vail West
Elevation Gain: 2,560 feet

Notes: This route follows roads all the way to the hut, but care must still be taken so as not to make a wrong turn onto another road, since snowmobiles have tracked out many of the road cuts in the area. Skins are not necessary on this route, most just use wax or their fish-scale skis. For the return trip, advanced skiers (watching the map closely) can cut a couple of the upper switchbacks.

Directions to Trailhead: Take I-70 to the main Vail exit (Exit 176), go to the North Frontage Road just north of the I-70 bridge, and go west 1.0 miles and take a right (N) on Red Sandstone Road. At .35 miles up the road, at a hairpin turn, you will see some parking, but continue up the road. At .7 miles there is parking at a hairpin turn, but continue left up the road to the snowplow turnaround (13S0380137E, 4390359N, 8,620 feet) at 1.3 miles to see if parking is available. Do not park in the turnaround, but along the road leading up to it. This is the most popular spot for parking for hutgoers.

Route Description: From the end of the plowed road, go up the wide road for 2 miles to a major road intersection of roads 700 and 786. Take the Lost Lake Road (786) to the right, do not go straight to Piney Lake and Lost Lake Trail. Follow Road 786 for 1.35 miles on a gradual uphill to the intersection of roads 786 and 719 at 9,700 feet

(13S0380517E, 4393992N). Stay right on Road 719 through the gate, following the 10th Mountain marked route. Continue on the road for another 3.6 miles to a somewhat confusing

The view out the front windows of the Eiseman Hut.

intersection of roads at a saddle-like area at 10,890 feet (13S0383763E, 4394734N). Stay straight (SSE) on the marked 10th Mountain route to where the road soon takes a sharp switchback left (N). Stay on the road heading N for another .4 miles to a sharp switchback trail to the right heading uphill the last 100 yards to the hut.

Reverse Route: From the hut, head out on the marked track NW for about 100 yards down to the road where you take a sharp switchback to the left (S). In another .4 miles the road takes a sharp switchback to the right (NW) and then soon reaches an intersection of various roads at a saddle-like area at 10,890 feet (13S0383763E, 4394734N). Avoid the road going up to the left and the one heading off to the right. Stay straight, making sure you are on the 10th Mountain marked trail. Continue on the long switchbacks and gentle grade of the road for 3.6 miles to the junction (at a gate) of roads 719 and 786 at 9,700 feet (13S0380517E, 4393992N). Continue straight (S) on road 786. In 1.35 miles you reach another road junction of roads 786 and 700. Take a left (E) and continue heading downhill on the wide road, watching and listening for snowmobiles, for the last 2 miles to the trailhead.

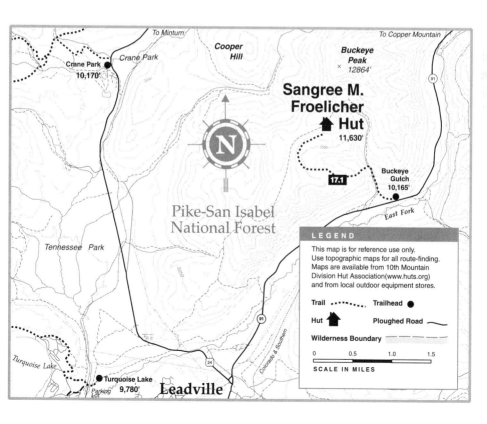

Chapter 17 • **Sangree M. Froelicher Hut**

This hut, located on the eastern slope of the Chicago Ridge north of Leadville, is named in honor of Sangree M. Froelicher who was killed in action in Italy in 1945 at the end of World War II. The hut is within a few feet of being the highest hut in the 10th

Elevation: 11,630 feet
Coordinates: 13S0391995E, 4353786N
County: Lake
Access: Highway 91, north of Leadville

Mountain Hut System, but is easily accessed from the Leadville area. A new addition, the Alpine Resource Center, has been added to the hut, and the entire hut and Center can be booked for educational purposes.

The ridge above the hut offers outstanding views and some good slopes for turns under the right snow conditions. 12,867-foot Buckeye Peak, lying to the north of the hut on the ridge, is a good destination for a ridge tour and for some good skiing.

17.1 Buckeye Gulch Trailhead to Sangree M. Froelicher Hut

Difficulty: Intermediate
Distance: 3.2 miles
Time: 3-4 hours up; 2 hours down
Text Map: p. 137
10ᵗʰ Mtn Map: None
USGS Map: Leadville North, Climax
Elevation Gain: 1,465 feet

Notes: The only route to this hut passes through private property and crosses a couple or roads at the beginning, so it is necessary to stay on the marked trail. The climb is steady, so skins should be used by most from the very beginning. In the higher open areas watch for the marked trail carefully as it traverses the last mile to the hut.

Directions to Trailhead: From the intersection of highways 24 and 91 at the north end of Leadville, go 4.7 miles north on Highway 91 and watch closely for a mostly hidden road on the left (north) side of the highway through the pine trees. Turn and follow this road a couple hundred feet to the marked public parking area (13S0393153E, 4351988N, 10,165 feet) for the trailhead. When coming down Highway 91 from I-70 by Copper Mountain Resort, go about 19.5 miles (depending on your odometer) and watch for the road in the pines on the right.

The Sangree M. Froelicher Hut trailhead parking off Highway 91.

Route Description: From the parking area follow the trail out of the end of the lot as it switchbacks steeply at first up through the trees and enters private property. The trail is well marked by blue diamonds as it cuts across a couple of roads and then follows a road cut somewhat steeply up the right side of Buckeye Gulch. At one mile, at the junction of two gulches, take a left (W) from Road 137 onto 137A which leaves Buckeye Gulch, crosses the creek and goes above the left side of the side drainage. After a couple of hundred yards the route switchbacks up to the left, rising above the drainage, then cuts back into the trees, climbing steadily on a well-marked route in the trees above the left (S) side of the drainage. In a little over a mile at 11,400 feet, the way starts opening up and the trail begins to bend right (N) above the head of the drainage. The trail works its way first NE and then mostly E below a ridge above on the left, through scattered patches of trees for the final traverse to the hut.

Reverse Route: From the hill above the hut head SW, watching closely for diamonds as the trail traverses below the ridge until it starts looping south and then east starting at 11,500 feet above the head of a drainage. The trail is well marked in the trees as it descends above the right (S) side of the drainage. A switchback through an open area drops you down to the creek which you follow to the intersection of roads 137A and 137. Here you go downhill (sometimes icy) on Road 137 above Buckeye Gulch until you enter private property and a well-marked trail down through the trees to the parking lot.

Chapter 18 • **Francie's Cabin**

Francie's Cabin, named in memory of the well-loved Breckenridge resident Frances Lockwood Bailey who died in a tragic plane crash in 1989, sits in a beautiful high country setting with access to some of the best touring from

Elevation: 11,390 feet
Coordinates: 13S0407650E, 4365985N
County: Summit
Access: Breckenridge

any hut. The short tour to lower Crystal Lake is a favorite for most of the hut visitors, as are tours in the Spruce Creek drainage. Be aware that the tours near the hut are in close proximity to avalanche terrain, so necessary precautions must be taken when touring and making turns.

The hut itself, managed by the Summit Huts Association, is quite modern as huts go, boasting a first-class detached sauna and inside compost toilets. To get to the hut, the hutgoer has a choice of trailheads, with the Spruce Creek Trailhead being the most popular due to the quick access it offers to the hut.

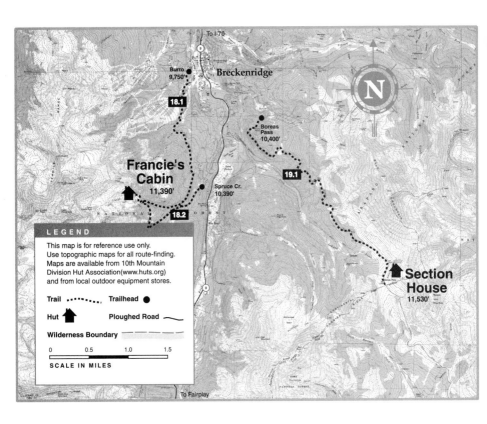

18.1 Burro Trailhead to Francie's Cabin

Difficulty: Intermediate
Distance: 4.1 miles (via Crystal Creek), 4.7 miles (via Spruce Creek Rd.)
Time: 4-5 hours up; 2-3 hours down
Text Map: p. 142
10th Mtn Map: None
USGS Map: Breckenridge
Elevation Gain: 1,640 feet

Notes: This is the standard, more scenic route to Francie's Cabin leaving from the Breckenridge Ski Area. However, access to the trailhead is a little involved due to lack of parking and the need to take a shuttle. Those who wish a shorter, quicker trip take the more heavily used route from the Spruce Creek Trailhead.

Directions to Trailhead: Park in the overnight parking at the Tailings Lot (Watson Lot) just off Watson Avenue in downtown Breckenridge.

Catch the Beaver Run shuttle bus to the Beaver Run Resort drop-off area and walk past the ski school area across the slope to the large US Forest trailhead sign for the Burro Trailhead (13S0409657E, 4369739N, 9,750 feet).

Route Description: Go into the woods following the trail cut. At the first fork, stay straight along the left side of a small gully. The trail, sometimes marked, winds up through the trees and comes to an intersection at 10,280 feet. Go left and follow the trail as it traverses S. Stay straight as a side trail drops down to the left at 10,400 feet. Three miles from the trailhead you will come to the steep Crystal Creek Trail at 10,620 feet going up to the right.

//If you have skins// go right here for the most efficient route to the hut. Go up on a steep climb to the right of the Crystal Creek drainage. In close to a mile, you reach an intersecting road going left (13S0407774E, 4365887N, 11,270 feet) and a sign prohibiting motorized travel. Continue straight. In about 200 feet you break into an open area where you head uphill to the right to the hut just over a small ridge.

//If you do not have skins// go straight on the Burro Trail for about 100 yards to Spruce Creek Road heading to the right. In .9 miles up the road you will come to an intersection where the Wheeler Trail goes straight, and a road cut goes up to the right (N). Go right uphill for about .8 miles to an intersection with a sign prohibiting motorized travel. Take a left. In about 200 feet you break into an open area where you head uphill to the right to the hut just over a small ridge.

Reverse Route: Go down the hill in front of the cabin, staying left in the open area to a left turn into the trees. In 200 feet take a right past a gate onto the road going over the Crystal Creek (going straight will take you down the steep Crystal Creek Trail) and continue on the road cut heading down along the right side of the Crystal Creek. In .9 miles from the cabin, just after a gate, at the intersection with the Wheeler Trail going right, go left to stay along the creek. The Spruce Creek gully will be off to your right.

After crossing Crystal Creek, in .1 miles watch for a narrow trail going left into the woods, marked by a blue diamond (13S0408936E, 4365573N, 10,655 feet). Turn left here onto the Burro Trail and in 100 yards you will cross the steep Crystal Creek Trail (13S0409123E, 4365687N, 10,620 feet). Stay straight. In about a mile, a trail breaks off down to the right (13S0409726E, 4366815N, 10,400 feet) to Spruce Creek Road. Stay straight. In another mile, the Burro Trail, marked by a blue diamond, takes a sharp turn down to the right at 10,280 feet (13S0409461E, 4368027N). Follow the trail as it winds down through trees, then follows the right side of a small gully to the right of the ski area. The trail exits the trees at the bottom of Peak 9 at the trailhead.

18.2 Spruce Creek Trailhead to Francie's Cabin

Difficulty: Intermediate
Distance: 1.3 miles (via Crystal Creek); 2 miles (via Spruce Creek Road)
Time: 2 hours up; 1 hour down
Text Map: p. 142
10th Mtn Map: None
USGS Map: Breckenridge
Elevation Gain: 1,000 feet

Notes: This short, popular route to Francie's Cabin offers two variant routes: the Crystal Creek Trail and Spruce Creek Road. For a shorter but steeper uphill route take the Crystal Creek Trail, otherwise follow Spruce Creek Road. For the downhill follow the Spruce Creek Road.

Directions to Trailhead: Drive south on Highway 9 (Main Street) through Breckenridge. Set your odometer at the stoplight at South Park Avenue. In 2.4 miles turn right onto Spruce Creek Road in the Crown subdivision. Follow Spruce Creek Road, bearing left at doubtful intersections to stay on Spruce Creek Road. Go 1.3 miles up Spruce Creek Road to a plowed parking area (13S0409581E, 4365818N, 10,390 feet) at Spruce Creek Portal.

Route Description: Go out the end of the parking lot on Spruce Creek Road (not on the trail on the left) for about 200 yards to a fork where the Crystal Creek Trail goes up steeply to the right and Spruce Creek Road continues straight ahead.

//Crystal Creek Trail// As you climb the steep Crystal Creek Trail, you quickly come to the crossing Burro Trail (13S0409119E, 4365681N, 10,620 feet). Continue straight on a steep climb above the Crystal Creek drainage on the right heading in a westerly direction. In close to a mile up the trail, you reach an intersecting road going left (13S0407774E, 4365887N, 11,270 feet) and a sign prohibiting motorized travel. Continue straight. In about 200 feet you break into an open area where you head uphill to the right to the hut just over a small ridge.

//Spruce Creek Road// If you stay straight on Spruce Creek Road, in .9 miles you will come to an intersection where the Wheeler Trail goes straight, and a road cut goes up to the right (N). Go right uphill for about .8 miles to an intersection with a sign prohibiting motorized travel. Take a left. In about 200 feet you break into an open area where you head uphill to the right to the hut just over a small ridge.

Reverse Route: Go down the hill in front of the cabin, staying left in the open area to a left turn into the trees. In 200 feet take a right past a gate onto the road going over the Crystal Creek (going straight will take you down the steep Crystal Creek Trail) and continue on the road cut heading down along the right side of the Crystal Creek. In .9 miles from the cabin, just after a gate, at the intersection with the Wheeler Trail going right, go left to stay along the creek. The Spruce Creek gully will be off to your right. After crossing Crystal Creek, in .1 miles watch for a narrow trail going left into the woods, marked by a blue diamond (13S0408936E, 4365573N, 10,655 feet). This is the Burro Trail for those going to the Burro Trailhead (see route 18.1). Otherwise continue on the Spruce Creek Road straight to the Spruce Creek Trailhead just ahead.

Frances Lockwood Bailey (Francie) and her guitar.

145

Chapter 19 • Section House

Elevation: 11,530 feet
Coordinates: 13S0416683E,
4362791N
County: Summit
Access: Breckenridge

The Section House and the adjacent Ken's Cabin are historic buildings, listed with the National Register of Historic Places, located at Boreas Pass on the Continental Divide above Breckenridge, Colorado. Ken's Cabin (the Wagon Cabin) was built in 1864 and the Section House was built in 1882 to house railroad workers that took care of this section of the railroad running from Denver to Leadville over Boreas Pass. The views in each direction from the Continental Divide are spectacular, but the weather can be quite cold and windy. All hutgoers should be prepared for extreme weather at this location. For the first part of the route up, there is a choice of taking the Boreas Pass Road or the more interesting, but slightly more difficult, Baker's Tank Trail.

19.1 Boreas Pass Trailhead to Section House

Difficulty: Beginner/intermediate
Distance: 6.5 miles
Time: 5-7 hours up; 3-5 hours down
Text Map: p. 142
10ᵗʰ Mtn Map: None
USGS Map: Breckenridge, Boreas Pass
Elevation Gain: 1,130 feet

Notes: The route from the trailhead to the Section House traditionally follows the Boreas Pass Road, originally a wagon trail, and later a railroad grade for the railway that ran from Denver to Leadville over Boreas Pass. The grade is easy, and even sometimes a little monotonous. For variety many people start up on the Baker's Tank Trail which leaves from the same trailhead. This narrow trail through the trees involves some climbs and a little more energy on the way up, and skiing skills if it is taken down. The trail ends at Baker's Tank on the railroad grade just about halfway up to the Section House, where it connects back to Boreas Pass Road for the final 3.4 miles to the hut. The recommendation is to take Baker's Tank Trail on the way up and to return via Boreas Pass Road. The lower part of the Boreas Pass Road is heavily used by walkers, snowshoers, and skiers on day hikes. The route offers good views of the Breckenridge Ski Area and the Continental Divide.

Directions to Trailhead: Take Route 9 to the south end of Breckenridge and turn E onto Boreas Pass Road at the stoplight. Follow Boreas Pass Road up 3.8 miles to a parking area (13S0412147E, 4368620N, 10,400 feet) where the plowed road ends. To get to the hut, you can continue out the end of the parking lot on Boreas Pass Road or take the marked Baker's Tank Trail which leaves from just above the parking lot.

Route Description: //Boreas Pass Road// Follow the railroad grade out the end of the parking lot. It passes through several rock formations and continues on a very gradual incline for 3 miles to Baker's Tank.

//Baker's Tank Trail// The trail, marked by occasional blue diamonds, heads up from the parking lot, a little steeply at first, winding through the woods as it gains the opposite side of the ridge from the Boreas Pass Road. Occasional side trails intersect; stay on the marked, and usually well-used, Baker's Tank Trail. After a narrow traverse along the SW

side of the ridge at about 2½ miles, the trail soon comes to a road cut where you drop down to the right a couple of hundred feet to Baker's Tank (13S0414208E, 4366501N, 10,900 feet) on Boreas Pass Road.

//Continuation for both routes from Baker's Tank// Continue up on the wide railroad grade as it gently ascends toward the Continental Divide. In just over 2 miles from the tank, the road breaks into the open with the flat open area of Boreas Pass ahead, cut into the Continental Divide. In bad weather this last mile can be windy and cold, and visibility may be bad. At the top of the pass the Section House and Ken's Cabin sit next to the road on the left, with an old railroad car on the other side.

Reverse Route: Follow the railroad grade N and NW from the Section House for the 6.5 miles back to the trailhead. If you wish to return via the Baker's Tank Trail (a little narrow and tricky on some of the

downhill sections), at
Baker's Tank take a right
around the tank, go uphill
a couple of hundred feet
and watch for the trail
going left off into the
woods. Follow the marked
trail to the trailhead, being
aware that side trails are
often created by
snowshoers and skiers.

Appendix 1 · **Equipment List**

General Equipment:
- Skis, snowshoes, split snowboards, poles, boots
- Backpack and daypack
- Climbing skins/wax kit
- Sleeping bag
- Headlamp with extra batteries
- Topographic maps
- Guidebook
- Compass
- Shovel
- Bivouac sack and ground cloth
- Fire-starting kit (matches, lighter, starting fuel, etc.)
- Survival kit
- First-aid kit
- Repair kit (including duct tape)
- Pocket knife
- Stove and pot (for emergency)
- Sunglasses and goggles
- Water bottles (wide-mouth)
- Sunscreen/Lip balm
- Food (each person should carry trail food)

Personal Clothing (wool or synthetics, no cotton):
- Parka
- Fleece Jacket/Vest/Shirt
- Windshell and windpants
- Knickers/Pants/Tights
- Socks/extra pairs
- Personal items
- Earplugs
- Long underwear top and bottom (foundation layer)
- Mittens, overmitts, and gloves/extra pari ski gloves
- Hat, scarf, balaclava, neck gaiter
- Leg gaiters
- Down booties/hut slippers
- Hand-towel and personal pillowcase
- Alarm wristwatch

Additional Recommended Equipment:
- Altimeter
- Probe pole
- Avalanche transceiver (also known as a "beacon" or "beeper")
- Ensolite or foam pad
- Cell phone (for emergencies only)
- GPS

Appendix 2 · **Directory**

Hut Reservations

10th Mountain Division Hut Association
1280 Ute Avenue, Suite 21
Aspen, CO 81611
970-925-5775
Website: www.huts.org
Email: huts@huts.org

Private Lodging (Fryingpan Valley)

Diamond J Guest Ranch (.3 miles from Montgomery Flats Trailhead
and 1½ miles from Norrie Trailhead)
970-927-4188
Double Diamond Ranch (3 miles from Montgomery Flats Trailhead)
970-927-3404

Hut Transportation

www.huts.org

Guides

www.huts.org

Maps

See www.huts.org (shop) for 10th Mountain maps
Contact local mountaineering stores or www.usgs.com for USGS
topographic maps

Weather

www.weather.com

Websites

Tenth Mountain Division Hut Association: www.huts.org
Summit Huts Association: www.summithuts.org

Avalanche Conditions

www.geosurvey.state.co.us/avalanche
www.huts.org
Aspen: 970-920-1664
Denver/Colorado: 303)275-5360
Summit County: (970-668-0600
Vail/Minturn: 970-827-5687

Forest Service Ranger Districts

Aspen: 970-925-3445
Eagle: 970-328-6388
Holy Cross: 970-827-5715
Leadville: 719-486-0749

County Sheriffs

In the event of an emergency, call 911 from any phone. If 911 does not work, call the appropriate County Sheriff's number.
Eagle County: 970-479-2200
Lake County: 719-486-1249
Pitkin County: 970-920-5310
Summit County: 970-668-8600

Local Mountaineering Stores

Aspen: Ute Mountaineer (970-925-2849)
Basalt: Bristlecone Mountain Sports (970-927-1492)
Breckenridge: Mountain Outfitters (970-453-2201)
Glenwood Springs: Summit Canyon Mountaineering (970-945-6994)
Leadville: Bill's Sport Shop (719-486-0739)
Vail/Avon: Christy Sports (970-949-0241)

Appendix 3 · **Hut & Trailhead Data**

HUTS	COORDINATES (UTM)	ELEVATION
Benedict Huts	13S0348341E, 4338121N	11,000 feet
Betty Bear Hut	13S0368549E, 4346304N	11,120 feet
Eiseman Hut	13S0384084E, 4394896N	11,180 feet
Fowler/Hilliard Hut	13S0389090E, 4372275N	11,540 feet
Francie's Cabin	13S0407650E, 4365985N	11,390 feet
Harry Gates Hut	13S0358004E, 4362456N	9,725 feet
Jackal Hut	13S0390054E, 4366191N	11,670 feet
Janet's Cabin	13S0394173E, 4368998N	11,630 feet
Margy's Hut	13S0352198E, 4348725N	11,300 feet
McNamara Hut	13S0349914E, 4344094N	10,395 feet
Peter Estin Hut	13S0358096E, 4369681N	11,200 feet
Polar Star Inn	13S0359602E, 4375975N	11,040 feet
Sangree M. Froelicher Hut	13S0391995E, 4353786N	11,630 feet
Section House	13S0416683E, 4362791N	11,530 feet
Shrine Mountain Inn	13S0393022E, 4377860N	11,225 feet
Skinner Hut	13S0373771E, 4347324N	11,680 feet
10th Mtn Division Hut	13S0380532E, 4358641N	11,415 feet
Uncle Bud's Hut	13S0378812E, 4351163N	11,400 feet
Vance's Cabin	13S0388050E, 4360105N	10,980 feet

TRAILHEADS	COORDINATES (UTM)	ELEVATION
Boreas Pass	13S0412147E, 4368620N	10,400 feet
Buckeye Gulch	13S0393153E, 4351988N	10,165 feet
Burro	13S0409657E, 4369739N	9,750 feet
Camp Hale	13S0385954E, 4365915N	9,260 feet
Crane Park	13S0385121E, 4356147N	10,170 feet
Hunter Creek	13S0343746E, 4340808N	8,380 feet
Lenado	13S0348835E, 4345412N	8,750 feet
Montgomery Flats	13S0355152E, 4356706N	8,240 feet
Norrie	13S0356989E, 4354742N	8,470 feet
Pando	13S0385619E, 4368082N	9,200 feet
Red Cliff	13S0383857E, 4375281N	8,830 feet
Red Sandstone Creek	13S0380137E, 4390359N	8,620 feet
Road 505	13S0363101E, 4351007N	9,110 feet
South Camp Hale	13S0386297E, 4364001N	9,350 feet
Spraddle Creek	13S0382681E, 4389169N	8,615 feet
Spruce Creek	13S0409581E, 4365818N	10,390 feet
Sylvan Lake	13S0350955E, 4371632N	8,585 feet
Tennessee Pass	13S0387030E, 4357844N	10,460 feet
Tennessee Pass/Ski Cooper	13S0387804E, 4357643N	10,570 feet
Turquoise Lake	13S0384448E, 4346969N	9,780 feet
Union Creek	13S0399945E, 4372836N	9,830 feet
Vail Pass	13S0395146E, 4376137N	10,650 feet
West Lake Creek	13S0361484E, 4383510N	8,340 feet
Yeoman Park	13S0355695E, 4374040N	9,085 feet

Bibliography

Dawson, Louis W. *Colorado 10th Mountain Huts & Trails,* 3rd ed., Basalt, Colorado: WHO Press, 1998.

Dawson, Louis W. *Colorado Backcountry Skiing,* vol. 1, Colorado Springs, Colorado: Blue Clover Press, 2000.

Litz, Brian. *Colorado Hut to Hut*, vol. 1, Englewood, Colorado: Westcliffe Publishers, 2000.

Messina, Scott. *Hiking and Mountain Biking the Hut System,* Aspen, Colorado: Tumbledown Publishing, 2003.

Perla, Ronald I. and Martinelli, M. *The Avalanche Handbook*, Seattle: University Press of the Pacific, 2004.

Yule, Leigh Girvin and Toepfer, Scott. *The Hut Handbook*, Englewood, Colorado: Westcliffe Publishers, 1996.

Index

R

Ranch Creek, 102-4
Ranch Creek Road, 103-4
Red Cliff, 112, 120, 122-23
Red Cliff Trailhead, 109, 112, 122, 153
Red Mountain Trail, 52
Red Sandstone Creek, 133-34
Red Sandstone Creek Trailhead, 136, 153
Red Sandstone Road, 136
Resolution Bowl, 106, 109-10, 117
Resolution Creek, 109
Resolution Mountain, 106-7, 109-13, 117
Resolution Narrows, 107, 111-13, 117
Resolution Road, 106-7, 117-18
Resolution Saddle, 107, 111-13, 117
Road 19, 81, 89
Road 104, 73, 76, 84
Road 107, 73-74, 76, 80-81, 84
Road 131, 90, 92, 94, 100
Road 400, 42-43
Road 416, 51-52
Road 505, 67-68, 71
Road 505 Trailhead, 67, 71, 153
Road 506, 43, 45, 55
Road 507, 43, 45
Road 700, 136-37
Road 713, 122-23
Road 719, 136-37
Road 728, 122-23
Road 747, 112, 122-23
Road 755, 103-4
Road 786, 136-37
Roaring Fork River, 22, 26, 32

S

Sangree M. Froelicher Hut, 138-40, 152
Sawatch Range, 102
Sawmill Park, 29, 34-36
Schuss, Jack, 102
Searle Pass, 127

Section House, 146-48, 152
Shrine Mountain, 115-16, 119-20, 124
Shrine Mountain Inn, 109, 112, 114, 116, 118, 120-26, 131, 152
Shrine Mountain Ridge, 114-16, 118-19, 122, 124
Shrine Mountain Saddle, 115-16, 119, 124
Shrine Pass, 116, 121-23, 125
Shrine Pass Road, 112-14, 116, 121-23, 126, 132
Silver Creek, 32-33
Ski Cooper, 91, 95, 97-99
Skinner Hut, 66, 68, 71-77, 79, 84-85, 152
Slide Lake, 88
Slim Jim Gulch, 39
Smith Gulch, 126, 130-32
Smuggler Mountain, 23-24
Smuggler Mountain Road, 22-24
South Camp Hale Trailhead, 102-4, 153
Spine Creek, 53-54
Spraddle Creek, 133-35
Spraddle Creek Trailhead, 134, 153
Spruce Creek, 28-29, 36-37, 141, 143, 145
Spruce Creek Portal, 144
Spruce Creek Road, 142-45
Spruce Creek Trail, 29, 35
Spruce Creek Trailhead, 141-45, 153
Squaw Creek, 59
Squaw Creek Saddle, 59
Stafford Creek, 126, 130-32
St. Kevin's Gulch, 79
Sugarloaf Peak, 127, 130
Summit County, 19, 151
Summit Huts Association, 8, 10 12, 127, 141, 150
Sylvan Lake, 39, 42, 47, 52
Sylvan Lake Trailhead, 42-43, 52-53, 153